HOW WE NAMED OUR STATES

★ ★ ★ ★

HOW WE NAMED OUR STATES

BY PAULINE ARNOLD
AND PERCIVAL WHITE

Criterion Books
NEW YORK
Published by Abelard-Schuman Limited

34631

Contents

There is no part of the world where nomenclature is so rich, poetical, humorous and picturesque as the United States of America. The names of the states and territories themselves form a chorus of sweet and most romantic vocables.

ROBERT LOUIS STEVENSON

How Places Get Named

Places need names, just as people do. They need names for easy identification and so that they may be distinguished from other places.

When people undertake to settle a new country, one of the first things they do is to identify the place where they are, where they have been, and where they want to go.

When the English settled on this continent the Indians had long since given names to the various tribes, the rivers and mountains they knew, as well as their camps and hunting grounds. Sometimes the new arrivals attempted to translate the meaning of the Indian names, but more often they twisted the Indian sound into their own tongue, spelling it by ear. Sometimes they discarded the Indian name entirely, choosing one in their own language to replace it.

Others as well as the English did this, too. The men from Spain who conquered the South and Southwest turned Indian names into Spanish or renamed places in their own tongue. So did the French explorers. Names also came into use because an important event took place on that spot or because of the appearance of the land, or because an explorer or a settler wanted to honor someone.

The naming of our states followed the same pattern. To some extent the names are the product of chance. Often a name just grew into usage until it was so well established that it was too late to change it.

The names of the original Thirteen Colonies were established long before the Revolution; these names were retained when they became states. As new areas were settled and application was made to Congress for statehood, the names chosen were usually those already in use. Later, when Congress named some of the states, the name chosen often bore no relationship to the area and sometimes disregarded the wishes of its people as well.

It has been said that if history books were destroyed the march of civilization could be traced through the names of the land. Our own country is an example. The names we gave to our rivers and mountains, our towns and villages, our colonies, our territories and to our states sprang from the movements of our people, the places from which they had come, the situations they had encountered. Naming places is part of pioneering. Once an area is accepted into the Union as a state its name is legalized, its beginning is past, its identification is fixed.

In this book we shall show how each of our states came to be named.

1. The Accidents of Naming

We have said that the naming of some of our states was a matter of chance. It is equally fair to say that the discovery of our country was an accident and its name an error.

What Columbus had discovered was not what he had set out to find. His first voyage, in 1492, landed him in what he called the Indies, for it was the Indies that he had sought. But the Indies he was seeking were in the Eastern Hemisphere; those he found were in the Western Hemisphere. He had come upon the Western World by accident.

On his second voyage, the following year, Columbus planted a colony on one of the numerous islands we now call the West Indies. Three years later he returned to Spain. In 1498 he again crossed the Atlantic Ocean, steering farther south until he came upon a great body of land – his first view of a continent. But it was the southern continent he had found, known to us as South America. He had missed the North American mainland entirely.

In the year in which Columbus first reached the Islands, Amerigo Vespucci left Italy and went to Spain, where he fitted out ships for navigators and finally went to sea himself. Amerigo was a great writer of letters, which were mainly devoted to exaggerating his exploits. His letters were written in Latin, which gave them authority with scholars.

In 1503 he wrote a letter claiming that his first voyage along the northern coast of what we know as South America was made in 1497, although it was later proved that he did not get there until 1499. He purposely put his trip two years ahead to make it appear that he and not Columbus was the first to find the continent.

Although Columbus had actually been there a year before Vespucci he was slow in making his claim in Latin to the scholars. The false claim of Vespucci was so convincing that an eminent professor of geography published a book in 1507, stating "Since Americus discovered it, it may be called Amerige; in other words, the land of Americus, or America." He went on to say that he preferred the form "America" since both Europe and Asia bore feminine names. He used that name on a map accompanying his book. The term was soon in popular use. A few years later, the professor changed his mind about the accuracy of his statement, but by that time the name America had been generally accepted throughout Europe, except in Spain, where they persisted in calling the new land the Indies even after they knew it was not.

The name of the man who had *not* discovered America was given first to the southern continent, for that was the land Columbus, and by self-assertion Amerigo, had reached. Thus we had "America" to the south, and "India," which Columbus thought he had reached, was the accepted name for the northern continent. The land to the south retained its name and the continent to the north, which at that time was considered merely an appendage to its southern counterpart, was later called North America. Not too long after the learned professor had incorrectly bestowed a name upon it, the entire land mass of the Western Hemisphere was known as America.

Two hundred and seventy-odd years later the name "The United States of America" was adopted by the Continental Congress of July 4, 1776. Our Founding Fathers, living in Thirteen Colonies strung out thinly along the eastern seaboard, practically appropriated the name *America*.

Today, when the world speaks of "Americans" it usually means inhabitants of the United States. We call ourselves Americans, without granting that those who speak Portuguese and live in Brazil, or those who speak Spanish and live in Argentina, have an equal if not, indeed, a better right to the name. After all, it was the *southern* continent that was originally named America. Canadians and Mexicans live along with us on the northern continent but they are not called Americans either.

Actually, we are almost forced to call ourselves by this broad term because otherwise the problem of what we should be called is almost insoluble. Other peoples of the world are known by the names of their countries: A Frenchman is from France, an Englishman from England, and so on. But it would certainly sound awkward to be called United Statesians, or United States of Americans. However unfair it seems to our neighbors, both north and south of our borders, we have had little choice in pre-empting the name "Americans."

The name "United States of America" has another, though minor, disadvantage. It does not lend itself to poem or song. It can hardly be chanted or shouted. The traditional three cheers of Hip, Hip, Hooray; Hip, Hip, Hooray; Hip, Hip, Hooray, United States of America, would leave us completely out of breath.

There was a rival name which actually preceded the one adopted by the Continental Congress. Philip Freneau wrote:

"What madness, heaven, has made Britannia frown?
Who plans or schemes to pull Columbia down?"

Not only would there have been justification for naming our nation *Columbia,* but it also had none of the disadvantages of a four-word title: it was short, precise, and provided a good name for its inhabitants. We could easily have found ourselves being called Columbians if Congress had been so inclined.

Some of our states were named almost as unreasonably as this, but most of them were logical enough. In the next chapters we shall examine these one by one, beginning with the original colonies on the east coast.

VIRGINIA
DELAWARE

2. *The Earliest Names*

Within fifty years after Columbus — and Amerigo Vespucci — had discovered the West Indies and the southern continent everyone seemed to be exploring the New World. Everyone, that is, except the English.

Ferdinand Magellan, a Portuguese navigator sailing in behalf of Spain, passed through the straits at the tip of South America. These were later named for him. Although he was killed in the Philippines, one of his ships continued around the world, proving not only that the world was round but also that the lands of North and South America were, indeed, a *new* world.

Ponce de León brought his ships to the east coast of Florida. Hernándo Cortéz with his Spanish soldiers conquered Mexico. Balboa crossed the Isthmus of Panama, to be the first European to view the Pacific Ocean. Hernándo de Soto crossed overland from Florida to Mexico. Spanish captains sailed along the whole coast of California. Francisco Coronado went as far into the interior as present-day Oklahoma. The French made settlements in Florida, while the Frenchman Jacques Cartier explored the St. Lawrence

19

River, providing the French with a claim to Canada. Verrazano, an Italian, sailed along the eastern coast of North America and was probably the first to enter New York Harbor.

The English had, as a matter of fact, employed one explorer, although he was an Italian in the service of England's king. This man, John Cabot, had reached the shores of Newfoundland or Nova Scotia about the time that Columbus had been going up the Orinoco River. But the English let any claims based on this discovery pass for a hundred years, since it was easier to get rich by plundering the Spanish ships as they were bringing home their treasure than it was to seek their own riches.

Nearly one hundred years after Columbus's time, many things began to happen in England. Queen Elizabeth had been on the throne for twenty-five years when Sir Humphrey Gilbert asked her for the right to plant a colony in Newfoundland. This she granted. But his ship was lost and nothing was accomplished. We know Sir Humphrey best as the man who shouted from the deck of his little ship battling for life in the waves, "The way to heaven is as near by sea as by land."

VIRGINIA

Another reason for remembering Sir Humphrey is that his half brother, Walter Raleigh, continued his work. The Queen gave Raleigh a new "patent," that is, a document authorizing him to go on with the plans for colonization. It is to this man that we owe our first settlements and the name of our first state.

Raleigh was of good family although not of the nobility. His home was in Devonshire by the sea, which gave him the opportunity to learn about ships even as a boy. He attended Oriel College, at Oxford, and became a well-educated and also adventurous young man. Successful as a soldier and as a sailor, he went to the royal court.

Elizabeth's court was showy, with elaborate dress, ornaments and entertainment. Men wore clothes of velvet and brocade, heavy with gold trimmings and jewels.

Queen Elizabeth was a domineering sovereign, jealous of her power but devoted to the welfare of England. She had never married; because of this she was called the Virgin Queen. Raleigh was young, tall, dark, handsome and with sparkling wit. It was no wonder the Queen showed him favors that made him one of the richest men of the kingdom. She bestowed on him a knighthood as well. As Sir Walter Raleigh he was a famous figure at her court for many years.

But all this was ahead of him when he planned the first voyage aimed at colonizing the new land. He himself did not go on the voyages but he outfitted and directed the plans, sending two ships to explore the Atlantic coast of the New World. They came in July of 1585 through what we know as Pamlico Sound to an island which the Indians called — as the explorers spelled it — Roanoak. (Today we spell it Roanoke and it is in what is now North Carolina.) This was probably the first name given any place on our shores by Englishmen.

When the captains of the two ships returned they brought with them reports of a sweet-smelling land, of an abundance of fish and of rich vegetation. They also told of the friendliness of the Indians. Raleigh took these reports to the Queen. He asked her to give a name to the new land. Her edict read, "The King is called Wingina, the country Wingandocoa, and now by her Majesty, Virginia." So was named the first territory in the United States, a virgin's name for a virgin land. The royal grant described it as "of huge and unknown greatness." Its limits extended in a 600-mile radius from Roanoke Island. That area would cover what are now eleven states, parts of ten others, and even a portion of Canada.

The next year Raleigh sent another expedition. Its stay on the land was short. Its leader aroused the hostility of the Indians and, his supplies being nearly exhausted, he quickly re-embarked for England.

Sir Richard Grenville turned up shortly afterward and left a garrison of fifteen men on Roanoke. Later Raleigh sent three ships with 150 colonists. The commander of the expedition was John White, who brought his daughter and her husband. Raleigh had directed him to land at Roanoke and pick up the garrison. He was then to go on and found the "Citie of Raleigh in Virginia" on the big bay to the north which we call the Chesapeake. But the city was never founded, since the captain of the ships sailed away leaving the colonists without supplies. Their plight became so cruel that eventually White himself set sail to get help, leaving behind him his granddaughter, Virginia Dare. She was the first English person to be born in what is now the United States.

It was not easy for White to bring help. England was fighting for her life against King Philip of Spain. It was not until the defeat of the Spanish Armada that the country was free to give attention to other matters. When White returned, four years later, he found no trace of the colony he had left there. But the land still carried the name given it by the Queen: Virginia.

Raleigh was never able to visit the new land. At first he was kept at court because he had become so valuable to the Queen that she would not give him permission to leave. Later, he lost the Queen's favor because he married one of her maids of honor without royal permission. As a result, both he and his bride were imprisoned in the Tower of London. But Elizabeth needed his services too badly to let him stay there indefinitely.

When James I came to the throne after Elizabeth's death in 1603, he clapped Raleigh back into the Tower again. Condemned to death on the scaffold, Raleigh was reprieved at the last minute by the King and returned to the Tower. He was later released to try to find gold in the Americas. The King wanted the gold, so Raleigh staked his future on the chance of finding it. But fortune was against him and he failed. Returning in disgrace he faced the old charges again and was at last beheaded.

Raleigh's faith in colonizing for England held firm throughout all his troubles. Twenty years after sending his first expedition to Virginia, although in disfavor and about to be sentenced to the Tower, he said, "I shall yet live to see it [Virginia] an English nation."

Although the colonies settled by Raleigh did not survive, a new Virginia colony founded more than twenty years later became our first permanent English settlement. This was Jamestown, on the James River, named for the man who by that time was King of England.

The year 1619 saw the first representative assembly in North America. The Virginia House of Burgesses was convened in Jamestown to help the governor and the council in reforming and remaking the laws of the colony. Since Jamestown had been settled only twelve years before and had barely survived its hardships, this was quite an achievement.

Jamestown did not, however, continue as the seat of government. In 1633 there began a scattered settlement called Middle Plantation, a few miles north of the site of Jamestown. Six years later it took the name of Williamsburg, probably from the man who founded the community — William Byrd. It was later made the capital of the province and retained the name Williamsburg. In 1693 James Blair obtained a charter for a college which was called the College of William and Mary, in honor of the English monarchs who then reigned jointly. This was the second college founded in the colonies, Harvard in Massachusetts being the first.

It was from here that the colony took the lead in supporting the oncoming struggle with England and it was here that the Fifth Virginia Convention met to pass the act that declared the colony to be free and independent.

During the latter years of the Revolution the capital was moved to the city of Richmond, farther inland at the head of navigation of the James River. This town, too, had originally been planned by William Byrd but was laid out by William Mayo a short time later. It was a beautiful site around a bend in the James River. It was called Richmond after the town in England that is on a similar curve of the Thames River.

It was here, at the second revolutionary convention of Virginia that Patrick Henry, Virginia-born patriot and orator, spoke the words which have rung down through the ages: "I know not what course others may take, but as for me, give me liberty or give me death."

Here the capitol building was built in 1785 from designs prepared by Thomas Jefferson using a model of the Maison Carré at Nìmes, France. Jefferson had so admired the building that he had the model made while he was in France as the American minister.

Richmond was the capital of the Confederacy from 1861 to 1865. When the war was over Virginia returned as a part of the United States and Richmond reverted to being capital of Virginia, which it still remains.

Virginia had originally been the name for the whole east coast, but as other colonies were settled it shrank until it included only the area immediately south of the Potomac. Yet Virginia remained the heartland of the new and rapidly growing country. Most appropriately its nickname became "The Old Dominion."

The Declaration of Independence was signed by seven Virginians, our Revolutionary Army was led by a Virginian, and four of our first five Presidents were Virginians. Thus the name which Queen Elizabeth had given to Sir Walter Raleigh for the new land was proudly borne.

DELAWARE

The little group which had settled Jamestown went

through a period of near starvation until a new governor arrived bringing supplies and recruits. He was Sir Thomas West, Lord de la Warr. During the two years he was in Jamestown, one of his captains, Samuel Argall, sailed north along the outer coast where he found the entrance to a large bay. He named the cape on the west for the Governor, running the French form of his name, de la Warr, into one English word — Delaware. From this the name spread; it became the name for the bay and for the mighty river draining into it. When the colonists came the name was there for them to use.

Even the Lenape Indians, who had lived there for generations, gradually gave up their own name for the river which they had called Kit-Haune, meaning simply "Great River," and took over the new name of Delaware. By some ironic fate their ancient name was lost; their tribe, their land and their river became known by the name of a man born in Gloucestershire, England, and bearing a French title.

Delaware was not to be settled first by the English. The Dutch came before them, moving southward from New York and New Jersey. Instead of using the name Captain Argall had given the point, the bay and the river, they called it the South River, marking the southern boundary of their claims. Then the Swedes thought they should have some of the new land and they, too, moved in along Delaware Bay. They wanted to call the river the New Sweden River. However, they stayed only a short time and the name was dropped.

The English did not make the strip of land along the Delaware their own until after they had taken New York and New Jersey away from the Dutch. But all the time they continued calling the river the Delaware River and so they were ready to call the new colony Delaware.

The boundaries of the colony were in dispute for a long time. Pennsylvania and Maryland both had claims. But in 1776 a state government was organized and the State of Delaware came into its own. One year later the town of Dover was designated as the state capital. It was originally named by William Penn. He was an educated man and may have known that "Dover" comes from an old word of the Celts (the first race in Britain of whose language we know anything.) Their word *dove* meant "black" and became the English name Dover, although why Penn wanted to name the town "Black" is hard to say.

Delaware has had a number of distinctions. It carries the second oldest state name in our country. It was a man from Delaware who rode eighty-six miles posthaste to Philadelphia to cast the deciding vote in the Continental Congress for the Resolution of Independence. The state was the first to ratify the Constitution of the United States. It is not insignificant that the motto of the state is "Liberty and Independence." Every act of Delaware confirmed this.

MASSACHUSETTS
MAINE
NEW HAMPSHIRE
VERMONT
CONNECTICUT
RHODE ISLAND

3. *England to New England*

Hundreds of years before Columbus coasted the shores of the New World the Vikings had settled in Iceland, explored Greenland and, under Leif Ericson "the Lucky," son of Eric the Red, had sailed down the northeastern coast of North America. The saga tells how he gave a "name after its nature" to each place — here Slateland, because of the slabs of slate, and there Woodland, because of the forests. When he found vines he called the place Vineland. Other voyagers sailed those coasts and wrote other names on their maps but no one is sure what language they were in or what place they described. Except for the maps and the tales that were told, the names vanished.

Then came Captain John Smith. Smith had the luck to arrive in the New World at a time when England was ready to colonize it. At the age of twenty-six, after ten years of adventure on land and sea, he embarked for Virginia with the group who were to plant the first English colony which would survive. On April 26, 1607, they "entered the Bay of Chesupioc". Going up the river, which they named the James, they founded the settlement of Jamestown.

Smith was a young man but he knew how to get things done. However, he was usually in some kind of trouble, for he would go after what he thought was needed and often trample on other people's feelings. He had been named a member of the Council appointed by the King to govern the colony but he had been under arrest on a charge of conspiracy on the voyage and was not allowed to take his seat on the Council. Fortunately for America he was cleared and his principal accuser was fined. It is fortunate because of the contributions to the new land which Smith was able to make. Without his ability the new colony would hardly have survived.

He might have remained in history without any other story told of him except that he was saved by Pocahontas, but for his great contributions. Pocahontas was the daughter of the Indian chief Powhatan, who had been friendly to the settlers until he condemned Smith to death for killing an Indian in the fight in which he was captured. As Smith was led forth to his death Pocahontas is said to have thrown herself upon him and begged her father for his life. Her father, who loved the young girl, gave in and Smith was adopted as a member of the tribe.

Smith went on to more and more adventures, but the life of Pocahontas was even more romantic if not so useful. She was later converted and baptized into the Christian faith and married John Rolfe, an Englishman. She went with him to England and was presented at Court, although King James I objected to the marriage. He did this not on the ground that she was an Indian but that Rolfe, a commoner, had dared to marry Pocahontas who was a princess, daughter of the "Mighty Prince Powhatan, Emperour of Virginia." Pocahontas lived out her short life in England where she died of tuberculosis.

It is said that she met John Smith again in England but this time he was poverty-stricken and neglected while she, as a princess, was next in precedence to the royal family.

Smith, in the meantime, had continued his explorations of Chesapeake Bay, which the Indians called — as Smith spelled it — "Chisapeak." He went as far up the Potomac as the present site of Washington. Although he was largely responsible for the survival of the colony at Jamestown he was also constantly in trouble with England as he too often took affairs into his own hands and defied the authorities. His most important exploration, and his last in America, was a fishing and exploring expedition in 1614 to the coast far to the north which was generally called North Virginia, being still a part of the original grant.

As he sailed along the shore and among the islands he learned to know the country, and he drew a map of the coast and noted the tribes and the settlements he saw. Smith always got along well with the Indians and the names he wrote down were usually those he learned from them. Still, he seems to have puzzled over what to call the whole coast. To name it as a part of Virginia evidently did not appeal to him, but to tie it in with the Old World from which he came seemed exactly right. He boldly wrote on his map the name "New England," applying it to the whole northern coastland. He also wrote a book which he called *A Description of New England.* The name seemed good to the English and to the King. Only six years later, when granting a charter to that land, the King wrote: "The same shall be called by the name New England in America."

MASSACHUSETTS

Another name Smith recorded came from the Indians. Smith wrote in his book that an Indian town was called "Massachuset." It appears that he made up his final form from two words the Indians used: "Mass-adchu" meaning "big-hill," but in one case followed by the syllable "seuck," making it mean "big-hill people" and in the other case followed by the syllable "ut" which made it mean "at big hills." Adding an *s* for the plural gave us the state name of Massachusetts which we have kept ever since.

Six years later came the Pilgrims. Sailing from Plymouth, England, in the tiny ship the *Mayflower*, the 102 persons aboard came to the bleak point of Cape Cod, on the inside of its hook, on November 11, 1620. We call the place Provincetown. Men from the ship explored the large bay for weeks in the cold and wind until they finally landed on the shore twenty-five or thirty miles opposite the bay where their ship was anchored. Finding a suitable spot, they brought the *Mayflower* across and anchored it in the new place where there was deep water for the ship, fresh water to drink, and a few cleared fields where the Indians had once grown corn. On December 21, they came ashore in what was the first colony in New England, known to us as Plymouth. It was named for the port from which they had sailed from England: Plymouth in the county of Devon.

There was a keeper of the records of the Plymouth colony who wrote of how the place appeared to these seventy-three men and twenty-nine women. After sixty-six days on the north Atlantic with its winter storms the weary travelers could hardly have been optimistic about their future. Nathaniel Morton, wrote:

"Besides, what could they see but a hideous and desolate wilderness, full of wilde beasts and wilde men? And what multitudes of them there were, they knew not: for which way soever they turned their eyes (save upward to Heaven) they could have but little solace or content in respect of any outward objects; for summer being ended, all things stand in appearance with a weatherbeaten face, and the whole country, full of woods and thickets, represented a wilde and savage hew."

Yet the Indians were not unfriendly. They even showed the newcomers how to plant corn and use the native products of the country. More settlers came and spread over the land. The Massachusetts Bay Colony arrived a few years later. John Winthrop, who had been elected governor of the colony, brought eleven ships and nine hundred settlers with him in 1630. They settled at the mouth of the Charles River (named for himself by young Charles Stuart before he became Charles I of England). John Winthrop called the place Boston but it took a final meeting of the Court to confirm this, as there were many different opinions. Boston was the name of a town in Lincolnshire from which many of the colonists had come.

From the beginning Boston was the seat of government of the Colony although the limits of the state — often called the Commonwealth — of Massachusetts were not really settled until 1819, when Maine was separated from it. Boston has remained the capital of the state ever since, although unlike most states its capitol building is called the State House.

The early colonists in Massachusetts were religious people, many of whom had left England in the name of religious liberty, but they rarely permitted anyone to worship as he pleased. Rather, they seem to have determined that the founders should set the rules for everyone else. Massachusetts is also famous for its persecution of witches, another aspect of the colonists' intolerance. More than one so-called witch was executed there.

But not everything was aimed at suppression. In 1636, only six years after the Massachusetts Bay Colony was formed under Governor Winthrop, the first school of College rank in the New World was founded. Harvard College in Cambridge, a part of Greater Boston, led the way for all the others in the country.

It was, of course, in Massachusetts that the patriots joined issue with the British when they revolted against the tax on tea and threw the cargo into the harbor; where Paul Revere rode to arouse the countryside to the coming of the British; where the "embattled farmers stood, and fired the shot heard round the world" at Concord Bridge. The first settlers in Plymouth and Boston have, in fact, been responsible for many important events in the United States of America. It might be more fitting if the state had a nickname that suggested this. It is sometimes called the "Bay State," which is suitable considering the outline of its coast and the size of Cape Cod Bay, but it conveys little of the great contribution its citizens have made to the country.

Two of the first six Presidents of the United States were from Massachusetts, the only father and son occupants in our history: John Adams, the second President, was followed by his son, John Quincy Adams, as the sixth.

MAINE

There are many theories as to how Maine came to be called Maine, but there are few facts to support them. Here are some hypotheses:

A report from the Smithsonian Institution informs us that Maine was the name of a former province in France and that the French explorers gave the name to this northern territory. An English Queen, Henrietta Maria, had been a French princess ruling over the province of Meyne and she may have inspired it. Another theory is that Mainlanders gave themselves the title of Main to distinguish them from people who lived on the hundreds of islands in that region.

Whatever its origin, in 1622 a charter declared that "all that part of the mainland" the grantees, Sir Ferdinando Gorges and Captain John Mason, "intend to name the Province of Maine." The name, however, was not much used. When the southern part of the land was given to Captain Mason he called his share New Hampshire, and in a later grant Gorges called his part New Somerset after the county where he lived in England. But at the time no one paid much attention to any of these names. Then the King took a hand and in 1639 his grant read:

"And we do name, ordain and appoint that the portion of the mayne land and premises aforesaid shall forever hereafter be called and named the Province or County of Mayne and not by any other name or names whatsoever."

Still, Maine had no settled boundaries. Massachusetts set indeterminate boundaries as it suited her own interests, claiming most of the Gorges and Mason grant. The Massachusetts court gave it still another name: Yorkshire. The name of Maine was supposed to disappear.

But the times changed. In 1665 three King's Commissioners entered Yorkshire and made quick work of the Massachusetts jurisdiction, restoring the old name given by the King. On the twenty-third of June of that year, as if his world had been turned topsy-turvy — as indeed it had — the clerk of the local court turned his books upside down and began to make the entries in the back, working forward toward the front, writing "Province of Maine" by order of the King's commissioners. Not until ten years later was the possession of the land by Massachusetts assured when at last the state purchased the Gorges portion of the original patents and thus obtained legal right to the northern country of Maine. This time it did not try to change the name, and until 1820 Maine was recognized as belonging to Massachusetts.

Maine was admitted to the Union in that year by consent of the parent state, the twenty-third to be admitted. One reason that this was done at that time was to balance it, a nonslave state, against the admission at the same time of Missouri, a slave state, thus keeping unchanged the division between North and South.

A host of explorers had sighted or visited the coast of Maine possibly beginning with the Norsemen and continuing until the time the English started to come in. In 1607 an attempt was made to place a settlement near the mouth of the Kennebec River under the direction of George Popham, for whom the place was named. Here a ship of thirty tons was built named the *Virginia*. She was the first ship to be built in America. The first *permanent* settlements made by the English were in the 1620's.

Maine was a frontier state, about half of its boundaries being with Canada, which made the area not only an exposed line but a battleground during the struggles of the English with the Indians and the French. Its own citizens, however, were also good at raiding the Canadian territory, which evened things up a bit.

The dispute over the boundary between Maine and the British in Canada lasted for a long time. At one point the battle over the area of the Aroostook River got so violent that it was called the "Aroostook War." Forts were erected, the Federal government sent General Scott to take command of the frontier, and war between England and the United States over a largely uninhabited region looked imminent. Wiser heads prevailed and a treaty (the Webster-Ashburton treaty) was finally signed in 1842 which gave to Maine the odd shape it now has, jutting way up into Canada.

When Maine was at last granted statehood, even though her northern borders were still in dispute, the capital city was Portland. Eleven years later Augusta, the oldest city on the Kennebec River, was chosen as the capital. This city was named, some years after the Revolutionary War, for the daughter of a prominent war leader and statesman, General Henry Dearborn. His daughter was Pamela Augusta.

The state is sometimes called the Pine Tree State, and well it may be. The availability of the tall straight trees served well the early shipbuilders of the country along the Maine coast.

New Englanders have a phrase which is unknown to the rest of the country. If they live in Connecticut, for example, they say Maine is "down East." They might also say "down to Boston." Now both of these places are — on the map — "up" from Connecticut although they are unquestionably "east." No true New Englander would ever speak of "going up" to Maine. The state is, however, the easternmost in the country. It is said that the first point in the United States the rising sun lightens is the peak of Mt. Katahdin, more than 5,000 feet above the coast and the lakes.

NEW HAMPSHIRE

Captain John Smith in his voyage along the New England shores in 1614 had reported favorably on the harbor at the mouth of the Piscataqua where New Castle now stands. Although Martin Pring preceded him in 1603 the earlier voyager may not have been so good at talking and writing about it, for Smith's book, *A Description of New England*, really brought the northern shoreline and the land back of it to the attention of those who mattered.

As we have seen in the story of Maine, the early histories of Maine and New Hampshire are bound together. The first grant was made in 1622 to Sir Ferdinando Gorges and John Mason. These two men soon divided it between them, one taking the northern, the other the southern part. The first was called the County of New Somerset, the other New Hampshire. Both names came from English "shires" or counties. Massachusetts claimed the whole area, giving it still another name — Yorkshire. But the English King always insisted that it be called the Province of Mayne.

While the name Somerset disappeared and Maine was used for the northern part, the people of New Hampshire fought for their name and their right to be a separate colony. Many years later this was confirmed by the King, but even after that Massachusetts asserted its claim. It took another fifty years before New Hampshire had her own government.

So New Hampshire had its name, confirmed by the King, for nearly a hundred years before it voted for freedom in 1775. The year before the Declaration of Independence was drafted, New Hampshire had declared for independence under its own provisional government. When the State Constitutional Convention met in 1788 to accept or reject the Federal Constitution forming the United States, there were some holdouts who apparently did not want to get tied up in anything but New Hampshire. In the end the state decided to go along, the ninth state to do so. It is not for nothing that the motto of the state is "Live free or die." New Hampshire had demonstrated its determination to do so for a long time.

Several years before the separation of the Colonies from England, a small town had been settled alongside the Merrimack River. By the time of the Revolution it had grown considerably. It had been given the name of Rumford, an English town known to the settlers. But when feeling against the British was running high the residents decided to change the name. Concord was substituted but nobody knows exactly why. It may, of course, have been named for the town of Concord in Massachusetts where the British troops first attacked, but perhaps not. A great many towns were named for an abstraction. Such names as Union, Providence, and Concord were common. In 1813 seven towns named Concord were listed by the Post Office.

Concord became the capital of the new state after it was finally established as a part of the new United States.

Granite was first mined in the early 1800's and remained an important product. Some reports say that this influenced the character of the inhabitants. Whether because of the stone or its people, the name "The Granite State" was adopted. Daniel Webster, one of its most famous native sons, not only typified the determination of his state but he was also a prodigious talker. It was said he could "talk down the devil." He was a unique American. When the Senate was debating the Compromise Bill on the entrance to the Union of free or slave states Daniel Webster was doing everything he could to hold the Union together. He said, "I was born an American; I will live an American; I shall die an American."

New Hampshire has another important event in its history. The first ship ever to fly the Stars and Stripes was built in the Portsmouth yard. It was sailed from that point by John Paul Jones in 1777, ready to help the American patriots on the high seas.

VERMONT

The boundaries of Vermont, unlike those of Maine, are clearly defined: on the east the Connecticut River marks the entire border with New Hampshire; on the west Lake Champlain is the demarcation between the state and New York for nearly two-thirds of the boundary.

It was down this waterway that Samuel de Champlain made his first explorations which led to his first sight of the upper Hudson River. Champlain claimed this territory for France and it remained in French hands for nearly a century and a half.

But the people from New Hampshire were beginning to push their way in, and in 1724 a blockhouse was built just across the Connecticut River, around which the town of Brattleboro developed. Still, it was not until the British had captured Canada in 1760 that migration from the East became heavy. Later the area was settled by so many people from Connecticut that it was sometimes called "New Connecticut." Massachusetts also sent its contingents, and New York finally brought suit to try to protect the titles to the land these immigrants from other states had taken up.

At this point Ethan Allen, who was in charge of the defense of Vermont, entered the scene. A military organization under Allen as commander was set up to combat this situation, by force if necessary. These men were called "The Green Mountain Boys" and not only won their fame in this situation but also in their later valiant campaigns in the Revolution.

The name of the state was derived from the French who had occupied it for so long. Since the state is mountainous and its mountains are green the French called it Monts Verts, meaning "Green Mountains." Officially this was transformed into the word Vermont by transposing the French words. The Green Mountain Boys were rightly called so.

When the Revolution started, the Green Mountain Boys, still under Ethan Allen, captured the fortress of Ticonderoga on Lake Champlain where, according to Allen's own words, he called upon the commander to surrender "in the name of the great Jehovah and the Continental Congress." This was the first aggressive act of the Americans in the war. Ethan Allen became the state's hero and has remained so to this day.

Allen was a blustery frontier hero, with boundless self-confidence and much shrewdness. He rarely lost a chance to assert both himself and his ideas. At one time he was so fixed in his opposition to New York that he carried on negotiations, indirectly, with the governor of Canada with a view to turning over Vermont to the British, although he gave as his reason a determination to defend the independence of Vermont.

When, in 1775, he went on an expedition against Canada. he was captured by the British and remained a prisoner for three years. Altogether, Ethan Allen was a hero to hold the hearts of Vermonters. Whether or not the motto of Vermont had been adopted in his time, his every action supported it.

"Freedom and Unity" was Allen's motto before it became that of his state, although *his* emphasis was sometimes more on "freedom" and less on "unity." He continued to serve Vermont until his death in 1789.

During the Revolution Vermont set up its own constitution and its own state government. Although not one of the original thirteen states, Vermont was the first to come in after the Union was formed, and was admitted in 1791.

Montpelier, the capital, is in beautiful country where two rivers intersect. The town, which was probably named after Montpellier, France, was first settled in 1787. Shortly after the state was admitted, this small charming town was created the capital. It has remained so ever since, nestled in its lakes and rivers and mountains, so typical of the State of Vermont.

CONNECTICUT

The great river which flows through this area and which gives the state its name was discovered by Adrian Block, a Dutchman, in 1614. The Dutch called this stream the "Fresh River" because Block had found the mouth of the river where the water was still sweet.

The Dutch worked their way eastward from their settlements in New Netherland in 1633 and established a fort on the river where Hartford now stands.

The Pilgrims in Plymouth had also heard of the river. It rises far north in New Hampshire, flowing south, so that even when it reached Massachusetts it was already a large river.

The name of the river is supposed to have been derived from the Algonquian word "Kwenihtekot," meaning a "long river place," so this name came from the north. But it is also recorded that those who first knew the river at its mouth found the Indians using words that sounded like "quienetucquet" or "quenticutt," the meaning of which was "long estuary" where the tide flowed back and forth. Finally the English wrote it as Connecticut, using the same name from its source to the sea. No one knows who first put in the extra *c* or why, for none who lived there, Indian or English, ever pronounced it. After a while people began to call the whole area by the name of the river.

Then began a rapid migration of people from Massachusetts. A trading post on the Connecticut River was established by people from the Plymouth colony. A preacher by the name of Pastor Hooker of Newtown (now Cambridge) took his entire congregation across Massachusetts and down the river with the unpronounceable name to settle in the town they finally named Hartford after the town many of them had come from in England. Three Massachusetts towns near Boston sent a number of their citizens who settled in Wethersfield, north of Hartford, and in Windsor, south of that point. A party of Puritans who had arrived in Boston only the preceding year sailed from there for the Connecticut coast and established the town of New Haven.

Most of those who left the Massachusetts Bay Colony did so because they disliked the strictness and narrowness with which it was governed. They were also antagonistic to the rigidity of the religious codes and the strictness with which they were enforced. However, they made few changes when they came to their new location: they drew up a "Plantation Covenant" which made the Scriptures the su-

preme guide in every civil as well as religious matter, and
they proved not much more tolerant than those they had
left behind.

They had laws for all their personal conduct, with severe
punishments for those who disobeyed them. The Puritans
in New Haven have left us some records of the rules by
which they lived. Among these are:

> "No one shall cross a river on Sunday but an author-
> ized clergyman."
>
> "No woman shall kiss her child on the Sabbath or
> fasting day."
>
> "Every male shall have his hair cut round accord-
> ing to a cap."
>
> "No one shall read common prayer, keep Christ-
> mas or saint days, make mince pies, dance, play
> cards, or play on any instrument of music, except
> the drum, trumpet, and jew's-harp."
>
> "No one shall be a freeman or have a vote, unless
> he is converted and a member of one of the
> churches allowed in the dominion."

Today we call these "Blue Laws" and Connecticut still has
many of them. It is sometimes called the "Blue Law State"
although it is more usually called the "Nutmeg State" because of the peddlers who went through the country selling
provisions and who were reported to sell wooden nutmegs
instead of the real spice, thus making themselves a nice
profit. The state has also been called "The Land of Steady
Habits," which perhaps goes right along with wooden nutmegs and no kissing on Sunday. Fortunately, the colonies of

Windsor, Wethersfield, and Hartford had more respect for freedom. They adopted the advanced idea that "the foundation of authority is in the free consent of the people." This principle served as Connecticut's first written constitution.

New Haven and Connecticut colonies were at first separate but they were united under a royal charter in 1662. Hartford was then the capital but it shared the honor with New Haven from 1701 until 1875. Since then Hartford has been the only capital.

Relations between Connecticut and its people and their motherland were no more satisfactory than were those of Massachusetts. A certain Sir Edmund Andros visited the colony in 1687 to undertake to invalidate the fairly satisfactory charter they had obtained earlier. But the Connecticut Yankees were too smart for him. They accidentally extinguished the candles at the meeting and the original charter was removed from the table in the dark. It is said that they hid it in a large oak tree, thereafter known as the Charter Oak. Unfortunately, Andros went right ahead and dissolved the existing government anyway, but it is a good example of Connecticut initiative.

RHODE ISLAND

In Massachusetts lived Roger Williams, who spoke his mind too freely to suit the Puritan fathers. Williams was educated for the Church and even served as a chaplain, but his condemnation of the state of ecclesiastical affairs in England made him so unpopular that he decided to emigrate to Boston. Opposed by the church authorities there, he went to Plymouth where he remained for two years as pastor. He was heartily disliked by the authorities of the Massachusetts Bay Colony for disagreeing with them on almost every point of church and civil rule. When these authorities were about to seize him and transport him to England he left there and founded the first settlement in Rhode Island in 1636. He gave the settlement the name of Providence. Williams later wrote, "Having in a sense of God's merciful providence unto me in my distress called the place Providence, I desired it to be a shelter for persons distressed by conscience."

Although Williams went to Providence "for the sake of his conscience" the Massachusetts General Court was glad enough to get rid of him. Williams had his own ideas of how a colony should be run. For one thing, it was his conviction that a civil court had no jurisdiction over a man's religious beliefs, insisting that in matters of conscience "man is responsible to God alone." He proposed that complete religious freedom should be maintained in his colony. It was hardly any wonder that Providence Plantation, as it was at first called, was regarded as "the sink of New England" by the Massachusetts settlers who believed that such freedom was heresy.

Another of his points of difference with the authorities was his conviction that the King of England had no right to distribute land in the New World but that it should be bought from the Indians, its rightful owners. His relation with the Indians in the new land was friendly; he learned their language and they trusted him. The Narragansets gave him a place to live on the bay.

Another troublemaker who followed Williams to Rhode

Island was Anne Hutchinson. She was a very bold and witty woman but her beliefs led her into dissension with the church and civil authorities in Massachusetts. She was tried several times and at last excommunicated. In 1638 she left the Massachusetts Bay Colony, doubtless with its blessing. She and others who believed in her established a settlement on the island of Aquidneck across Narragansett Bay from the mainland.

There are varying tales as to how the state got its name.

When the Italian explorer, Verrazano, reported sighting the large island off the mainland he said it resembled the Isle of Rhodes in the Mediterranean Sea.

One historian says the name originated with Adrian Block, who, writing in Dutch, called Rhode Island "Roodt Eylandt," meaning red island, because of the fiery aspect of the place caused by the red clay. The spelling Rhode in English is to be expected, as it was in accordance with the standard way of spelling the syllable.

Later it was decreed that the island of Aquidneck, where Anne Hutchinson had settled, should be called Isle of Rhodes or Rhode Island. It seems extraordinary to take a name from the Mediterranean but this may not have been its real source, since it was at first spelled Road Island, as though it were an island where ships "rode" to their anchors. Finally the official name, confirmed in 1776, became "Rhode Island and the Providence Plantations."

During the Revolution the British occupied Newport but the colonists made much trouble for them through the use of privateers. Even as early as 1772 the Rhode Islanders burned the English revenue vessel *Gaspee*. They were always a strong-minded people. The state's nickname has been "Little Rhody," but its people had the courage of giants.

Rhode Island did not send delegates to the Constitutional Convention and seven times voted against ratification. It gave in only when Congress passed a tariff act under which Rhode Island was treated as foreign territory. They found they had either to join or go it alone. The motto of the state is "Hope," but this apparently did not apply to the last alternative.

The city of Providence has remained the capital of the state not only since it was admitted to the Union as the thirteenth state but ever since Roger Williams founded it. It is a long time for one city to lead a state.

MARYLAND
NORTH AND SOUTH CAROLINA
GEORGIA
DISTRICT OF COLUMBIA

4. Queens and Kings

Nearly fifty years after the first English settlement at Roanoke the huge area originally called Virginia was still wilderness. But a few more English people were becoming interested in living there.

Its southern portion had been explored by men from Spain, France, and England. Both the Spanish and the French made early settlements but they all failed as, of course, did the first English colony at Roanoke. Then the London Company was organized for colonization. In December 1606 the first shipload of immigrants under the new company left England, but after nearly twenty years the company failed and the whole area of Virginia passed to King James I. The King was all set to annul the liberal charter of the colony under which it had been governed but he died before this was done.

Soon afterward King Charles came to the throne. He continued the self-government principles and thus created a form of lawmaking assembly that became a model for colonies not yet in existence.

Soon afterward he cut off from the Virginia grant two

great provinces. The first of these lay to the south of what we now know as Virginia. The second was given to George Calvert, Lord Baltimore. It lay to the north and east of the Potomac River.

MARYLAND

Little was done to settle or improve the southern lands, but Lord Baltimore acted vigorously for his province. One of his purposes in setting up the colony was to offer a place where there would be freedom for everyone to practice whatever religion he wished. Lord Baltimore had been converted to Catholicism, but both Catholic and Protestant groups were being persecuted in England. The new proprietor wanted to provide a community where people could live in safety and freedom, without friction among themselves.

The story goes that when, in 1632, Lord Baltimore went to the King, Charles I, to get a name for his colony he wanted to call it Crescentia. This appealed to him because it meant "growing" or "increasing." He probably felt that this name would be a good omen. However, when his Lordship drew up the draft of the charter he tactfully left the name blank. The King, seeing the blank space, asked what name should be placed there. Lord Baltimore replied that he wished a name which would honor the King, although the feminized form of Charles had already been granted to the lands to the south — Carolina.

Apparently the King liked using the names of his family for new lands: he had already used those of his mother and his sister in New England when he named two peninsulas Cape Elizabeth and Cape Anne. He now added that of his wife, Henrietta Maria, youngest daughter of the King of France.

"Let us," he is reported to have said, "therefore give it a name in honor of the Queen. What say you to Mariana?"

Baltimore presumably still had his eye on Crescentia and may have demurred a bit but the King finally said it should be called Terra Mariae (in Latin) or Maryland in English. To make this final he added, "So we name it and so we will it to be named in the future."

Lord Baltimore died as the charter was about to be signed but his son Cecilius or Cecil inherited the province and admirably carried on the work of his father. He sent a younger brother, Leonard, to be the first governor. The colonists came in two boats most suitably named for the purposes for which the colony was founded — religious freedom. The boats were the *Ark* and the *Dove*. Although the founder, Lord Baltimore, had left the naming of the province to the King, he has been more than honored in the large city bearing the name.

Not long after the province had been given to the Calvert family, another early settlement was made by Puritans who came to live on the south bank of the Severn River, on the shore of Chesapeake Bay. They named their community Anne Arundel Town, after the wife of Cecilius Calvert, but this was an awkward name to pronounce. As time went on it was probably shortened to Anne, and in 1695 it was formally changed to Annapolis. The ending *polis* is the

Greek word for city and they added it to the Anna in a sensible way.

The people of Maryland were so devoted to the ideal of self-government that they frequently resisted not only the royal governor, Parliament, and the King but even the dictates of the Continental Congress. They vehemently resented the British actions: only a year after the famous Boston Tea Party Maryland staged her own by forcing the owner of a tea-laden ship to burn and sink his vessel at Annapolis. Indeed Maryland soldiers fought so vigorously in the War of Independence that their description "troops of the line" became the state nickname as "The Old Line State."

Annapolis became the capital of the state when the Constitution went into effect, while the name of the county remained Anne Arundel. Maryland joined the other colonies when, in 1788, it adhered to the new Constitution, the seventh state to do so.

One other contribution from Maryland deserves to be added although it took place in the War of 1812, twenty-five years after the United States was formed. British warships were attempting to capture Baltimore by working up the river from Chesapeake Bay. To do so they had to pass the fort which was guarding the entrance. Both sides were firing heavily. On one of the British vessels was Francis Scott Key, a Washington lawyer who had been captured and imprisoned by the British. All through the night he watched the flag with one thought in mind: if the flag still waved over the fort at daybreak Baltimore would be saved.

The flag was waving proudly when the sun came up and Key had put new words to an old English melody.

> Oh, say can you see
> By the dawn's early light?

NORTH AND SOUTH CAROLINA

After the London Company failed and Virginia was returned to the King, Charles I made an extensive grant of land south of Virginia to his Attorney General, Sir Robert Heath. Some say that Sir Robert asked for it and begged to be permitted to name it for the King; others say that the King made the grant on condition that it should be named for him, wishing it to be called Carolana or Carolina. In 1629 he established the name in the charter:

> Know that we of our free grace, certain knowledge and mere motion do think fit to erect the said Region, Territory and Isles into a Province, and by the fullness of our power and kingly authority for us and our heirs and successors we do erect and incorporate them into a province and name the same Carolina.

In any case the grant, as had the previous one, lapsed for want of efforts to people the region.

In 1663 Charles II granted another charter to eight friends of his. These were nobles and men of means who had no interest in the colony except to get money from it. They never visited it and soon ceased to pay any attention to it. The name Carolina was confirmed in this grant.

Fortunately, the people of the colony gradually grew in numbers as well as in prosperity. A slow but steady stream

of settlers came down from Virginia and stayed in the
northern part of Carolina. These were mostly poorer people
who found the aristocratic areas of Virginia not to their
liking. The southern colony grew wealthy through its agriculture and its importation of slaves. It became a center of
elegance and luxury with great plantations, whereas in the
north small farms prevailed. Although the northern colony
was noted for its democratic conditions in contrast to the
upper-class dominance of the southern part, it lacked good
harbors and important natural resources.

Thus different types of settlements were founded in the
two portions, so that about 1690 the northern part began to
be called North Carolina to distinguish it from the southern
part, which they called South Carolina. Since the original
grant carried the name Carolina it seemed wiser not to
create a new name for either part. Some years later the
two areas were officially divided but the exact boundaries
were not formally established until many years after the
Revolution.

The first and chief settlement of Carolina was made in
the south in 1670. Appropriately, it was named for the King
who had been so generous to his eight friends. They called
the settlement Charles Town. This later became known as
Charleston. It was the governmental center of the province.
When the treaty with the British ended the Revolutionary
War, Charleston was named the capital of South Carolina,
but three years later the state purchased land in almost the
geographical center of its area for a new capital city. There
then arose considerable debate as to what the new town
should be named. The District of Columbia had not yet

been established but the people of South Carolina fore-stalled it by adopting the name Columbia for their capital city. And that is what it is called today.

North Carolina also wanted a place for its capital that would be central to all its people. In 1788 it followed the example of the south and sought for "an unalterable seat of government." It purchased a thousand acres of land in the middle of the state. In a suitable tribute to the man who had made possible the first landing in Roanoke in what became North Carolina, they named it Raleigh.

A high degree of difference between the peoples of the two states had developed even in the early days. These remained as they began, differences in the terrain, the resources, and in the people who came to settle there.

But both states have cultivated a belief in independence and the willingness to fight for it. Both divisions of Carolina heartily supported the fight for national independence. In fact, both were ready for it before Congress was prepared to declare it.

North Carolina men, popularly called "Tarheels," fought in every major operation with Washington. It is said to have been called the Tarheel State because, as some residents recall, tar makes you stick better in a fight. It could also have been called the Old North State as it was named in a poem known to most North Carolinians:

Here's to the land of the Long Leaf Pine
The summer land where the sun doth shine
Where the weak grow strong and the strong grow great
Here's to our home, the Old North State.

South Carolina men had to fight the Spanish, the French, and the Indians. Their struggle to gain possession of the Sea Islands along their shore went on for generations. Their defiance of the British was second to none. South Carolina was the eighth state to ratify the Constitution and North Carolina the twelfth.

GEORGIA

For fifty years no other colonies were planted in the New World. The Spanish still held on to the Florida peninsula and were in frequent conflict with the British in South Carolina. After a successful battle in the early 1700's, the British were able to land and displace the Spanish. As a result, the seacoast to the south of South Carolina and the land across the Savannah River to its west were opened to the British.

At this point General James Oglethorpe stepped in to become what might be called the patron saint of the new area. He organized colonies, was a member of Parliament and a philanthropist. Since he had long given his attention to the plight of men in the English debtors' prisons, he now conceived the plan of preparing a haven for them. He wanted to give them a chance to start a new life by providing a place to which they could emigrate.

Many clergymen, noblemen, and others supported the plan. In 1732 the King, George II, chartered the Georgia "Trustees" to plant a colony between the Savannah River and Florida. The new grant was almost automatically called Georgia in honor of the King. Since three kings named George ruled England for over a hundred years, the choice was suitable. Although the third George, who was on the throne during the American Revolution, was no friend of the American patriots, Georgia did not consider changing its name.

The next year, Oglethorpe, who had been appointed governor, arrived in Charleston with more than a hundred colonists. Only a small proportion of those who came in the following years were from the debtors' prisons but others from England, Scotland, and Germany made up the population of about nine thousand, one-third of them slaves, that lived there thirty years later.

The British still had a problem with the Spaniards. Oglethorpe, during the last ten years of the English war with Spain, which ended in 1748, had the problem of coping with Spain in the New World. By that time the English were in control and the success of the new colony was assured.

Savannah, at the mouth of the Savannah River, was laid out and became not only the major seaport but the center of government. Georgia did not hesitate in her allegiance to the new land and joined the new Union in 1788 while Savannah was still the capital. It was also the fourth state to ratify the Constitution. However, as the state grew and the population spread to the west, it became clear that Savannah, on the seacoast, was not ideally situated to be the capital. New towns had grown up all over the state. One of these, well to the northwest of the state, grew rapidly after the railroad came in. It was called, simply, Terminus, because it was the terminal point of the Western and Atlantic Railroad. When the government decided this location would be ideal for the new capital they also sought a new name. The first thought seems to have been to call it Atlantic, from the name of the railroad, but it was nowhere near the Atlantic Ocean. Then, probably remembering the old custom of using a feminine form for names (as had been done in changing George to Georgia), someone suggested Atlanta, which was adopted. But Savannah served as a capital for a long, long time; it still remains the chief seaport and the oldest city in Georgia.

DISTRICT OF COLUMBIA

The First Continental Congress met in Philadelphia on September 5, 1774. The second meeting was also held in Philadelphia. Other Continental Congresses were held in Baltimore; in Lancaster, Pennsylvania; in York, Pennsylvania; and again in Philadelphia. In 1781 the Articles of Confederation provided for the continuance of Congress and it became known as the Congress of the Confederation, under which name it had an even more wandering life. It met in Philadelphia; in Princeton, New Jersey; in Annapolis, Maryland; and in Trenton, New Jersey, with five sessions held in New York City. The Congress of the United States, established by the ratification of the Constitution, then met in New York and in Philadelphia.

It became evident that a more permanent site must be chosen, not only for the convenience of the lawmakers and the President and his Cabinet but to provide the proper setting of dignity for the government of the United States.

A site on the Potomac was eventually agreed upon, after many disputes among various sections and existing cities of the country. The area finally decided upon was carved out of the states of Maryland and Virginia, although that of Virginia was returned nearly fifty years later. The site was chosen by President Washington, and it was he who selected Pierre Charles L'Enfant, a French engineer, to design the city.

It was apparently named by the three men who were appointed by the President to superintend the building of the federal capital. These men informed the President that they had determined upon the name "The Territory of Columbia" for the area and for the federal city they had chosen "The City of Washington." Their choices were apparently never questioned. What could be more suitable than the honoring of the discoverer of America — Columbus — and the Father of his country and its first President — George Washington?

The Capitol and the residence of the President were in use when the British burned the city in 1812. It was from the white paint applied to cover fire damage that the President's home came to be called the White House.

Although initially called a territory, it was described as the District of Columbia at the first assembly of Congress in the new capital on November 22, 1800, and so it has been called ever since. Among tens of others of our states which began as territories, this is the only territory that will never become a state. It belongs to the nation as a whole.

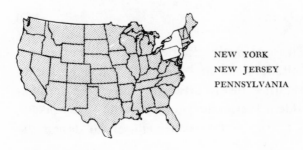

NEW YORK
NEW JERSEY
PENNSYLVANIA

5. Penn, York and Hudson

In the early explorations, rivers were the means by which new lands were found and explored. Rivers also were "roads." They were not only the chief means of travel, but they also served as boundaries of the lands claimed by the different nationalities of colonists. The Middle Atlantic section of the east coast of America abounded in large rivers.

In the fall of 1609 Henry Hudson entered a great bay and, in his ship the *Half Moon*, sailed nearly 150 miles up its river, anchoring for some days. Hudson was sailing for the Dutch, who called him Hendrick, but he was an Englishman. He did not name the river which was later to bear his name, calling it in his report only "The River."

Two years before that Samuel de Champlain had come down from the St. Lawrence River along a valley of lakes and rivers. He came upon "The River" only about a hundred miles above the part later reached by Hudson.

In the same year in which Champlain was traveling south, an unknown English voyager entered "The River," but did not explore beyond the large bay we know as

New York. Hudson may have had access to some of his maps.

Even before that time, in 1524, Verrazano, an Italian exploring for the French, had entered the bay.

(Hudson had also entered what we know as Delaware Bay before he found "The River" but he did not name it. A few years later a Captain Argall, sailing with Lord De la Warr to Jamestown in Virginia, entered the bay and named its western cape Delaware from which came the name of its river.)

Then came Captain Adrian Block with another captain who spent the winter of 1613 at the spot where Henry Hudson had anchored a few years before. The next year he sailed through the strait to the east of Manhattan Island. He called the strait the East River and from it he sailed on out into the open sound. When he came to a large river on the mainland he called it the Fresh River, to distinguish it from one he had explored the previous year.

The explorers from the Old World were converging on the New by the aid of its rivers, opening up access to the land as they went.

Some of these river names were modified as colonists began to come. In a short time the English were established in the northern parts of the coast, working their way south and west. They were also in Virginia and moving northward. The Dutch sent their first permanent settlers up the Hudson River to the present site of Albany, moving down the river to its mouth, across it to the west and the south.

So the English called Block's Fresh River the Connecticut, from its Indian name, while the Dutch continued to call it as a Dutchman had named it. The Dutch called the English-named Delaware the South River, because it was the farthest south of all the rivers they knew. They called the river on which Hudson had sailed the North River, as a counterpart to their South River and because it ran so far to the north. The Dutch never used the name Hudson. It was left for the English to do that. The Dutch called it just "The River" or the North River or the Great River. Officially the Dutch named it Mauritius, but a Dutch mapmaker wrote Groote Rivier.

As time went on some of these rivers became the boundaries between the lands which became states. The Delaware separates the State of Delaware from New Jersey; farther north it separates New Jersey from Pennsylvania, and at its extreme north it runs between New York and Pennsylvania. The Hudson separates New York and northern New Jersey. As it continues north it stays within the boundaries of New York.

NEW YORK

While the English were busy in New England the Dutch were at work on both sides of the Hudson and as far south as their South River, the Delaware. They called the area New Netherland. In 1624 they made their first settlement in the new land. Some remained on the island of Manhattan and others went on to a location near what is now Albany. Two years later they bought from the Indians the island of Manhattan for, it is said, twenty-four dollars. They called their settlement New Amsterdam.

The charter limits of New Netherland ran from the Connecticut to the Delaware and west into the unknown. But the settlements were scattered and the settlers were dissatisfied with the governors sent out by the Dutch West India Company. Their colonization was not too successful.

The English, however, were expanding their colonies, moving down into Connecticut to within forty miles of Manhattan and crossing over to settle on the eastern end of Long Island. The English had never given up their title to the whole coast. They claimed that the Dutch colony was within the formal bounds of both New England and Virginia. The time came when they were ready to take over from the Dutch.

In 1664 Charles II determined to take action. Disregarding the fact that he did not hold possession of thousands of square miles of it, he made the land claimed by the Dutch into an English province which he gave to his brother James, the Duke of York.

The Duke reacted immediately. He appointed Captain Richard Nicolls his deputy-governor and sent him over with three or four frigates and a considerable number of soldiers. Nicolls arrived off New Amsterdam and demanded its surrender. The Dutch Governor, Peter Stuyvesant, found himself up against not only the British troops but also the English from Connecticut and Massachusetts, as well as those who had moved on to Long Island. Far worse than that, his own people gave him little support. They were apparently determined to help the English wipe out the rule of the Dutch West India Company.

The Dutch Governor ordered the guns of the fort to open fire on the English, but his own people dragged him ignominiously away before the artillery could be fired. In the face of this the Governor surrendered. When, a short time afterward, the forts on the Delaware also fell to the British, their flag flew from Maine to the Carolinas.

The old problem of river and place names in two languages was also gone. The Hudson, the Connecticut, and the Delaware would henceforth be called by the names the English had given them. To this day the inhabitants of Manhattan usually refer to the river running west of their city as the North River although it runs parallel to the one on the other side of their island which is still called the East River.

Colonel Nicolls lost no time in renaming his conquest. On the very day of the surrender he declared New Netherland and New Amsterdam both to be New York. The name, of course, was to honor his patron, the Duke of York. He also honored a still older version of the Duke's name, probably without knowing it. The town of York in northern England had a long history. Called Eburacon, meaning "the place of the yew tree," it had been conquered by Romans, Angles and Danes. Each time its name was modified or altered. The Romans called it Eburacus. Eoforwíc was what the Angles called it, meaning "place of the wild boars." Three hundred years later the Danes, also called Vikings, made it over into their own language and produced Yorvik or Iórvík which, in the course of time, was whittled down to York.

In 1327 Edward III became King of England. He preempted the ancient title of the great northern city and county of York for one of his sons, whom he created the first Duke of York. In the seventeenth century this title was bestowed upon James, second son of Charles I, brother of Charles II. Thus it came about that New York drew its name from a town first known by the Celtic word for yew tree, but more immediately from a not very admirable duke.

Colonel Nicolls also bestowed the Duke's name on the town that the Dutch had called Fort Nassau and also Fort Orange but which the people called Beverwyck, meaning "Beaver-town," because it was an important fur trading post. The Duke's Scottish title was Duke of Albany, and so the town was named.

After the Revolutionary War ended Albany was at the crossroads of the newly developing nation. Before it was chosen as the capital the Provincial Congress met at White Plains, where they ratified the Declaration of Independence. It also met in Kingston where it voted in favor of the Constitution after considerable delay and opposition. It was the eleventh state to do so. Sometimes it met in Poughkeepsie, but in 1797 Albany was designated as the capital of New York State.

In the meantime a greater honor had come to the state. On an April morning in 1789 New York's streets, its harbor, its windows were jammed with the masses who had come to watch a well-known noble figure on the balcony of the Federal Building. George Washington was being inaugurated as the first President of the United States. In a sober voice the oath was stated to him:

"I do solemnly swear that I will faithfully execute the Office of the President of the United States, and will, to the best of my ability, preserve, protect and defend the Constitution of the United States."

Laying his hand on the Bible George Washington said: "I swear — so help me God!"

It may seem a little arrogant that the state has taken to itself the secondary name "Empire State." Perhaps it is because it has the largest city, the most wealth is congregated there, and it is the financial center of the country.

NEW JERSEY

The Dutch considered their province of New Netherland to extend south to Delaware Bay and west almost indefinately. It was cut neatly in two parts by the Delaware River, running north and south. In the same year that Captain Nicolls ousted the Dutch and gave the Duke's name to New York the King gave the land the Dutch had claimed west of the Hudson to two of his friends — Lord Berkeley and Sir George Carteret. Nicolls wanted to continue the application of the Duke's title — Duke of Albany was his Scottish title — by naming it Albania, but the proprietors had their own ideas. Carteret came from the island of Jersey which lies off the English coast. The Duke had found refuge there during some troubled times and might also appreciate the name Jersey. So the charter was made out as Nova Caesarea, in Latin, or New Jersey, in English.

This land, undefined as to its western boundary, was settled largely by English in its eastern part, while from the other side of the Delaware it was settled by Quakers. The two parts began to be referred to as East Jersey and West Jersey. Eventually the two proprietors divided their land, Berkeley taking the western part and Carteret the eastern.

Twenty years later the eastern part was also purchased by Quakers from the Carteret heirs. By this means the final boundaries of what was to become the State of New Jersey were defined: its western boundary was the Delaware River, its eastern the Hudson and the Atlantic Ocean.

Surrounded by water on all but its north side, with almost its whole east side protected by the reef outside Barnegat Bay, the state was one of the earliest to be developed in all its parts because the areas could be reached so easily. But its southern and southwestern lands are fertile and level while its northwestern areas are scenic and mountainous. Good farms grew up in all of these parts, so that when it became The Garden State the name was well chosen.

In the beginning, the colony had chosen as its first seat of government a settlement to which the governor gave the name of Elizabeth. Presumably this was in honor of Sir George's wife, Lady Elizabeth. But another capital was to come. There had long been a large estate in southern New Jersey on the bank of the Delaware River owned by a William Trent from Philadelphia. As a settlement slowly grew up there it probably became Trent's Town. Eventually it became known as Trenton, which was the scene of Washington's historic withdrawal across the river in the middle of winter, thus saving the remnants of his army. It later became the scene of his triumph when, on Christmas night, he recrossed the Delaware with three columns of soldiers of which only one, including Washington himself, reached the town. By advancing eight miles through a storm of sleet, he captured the Hessians, and took a thousand of them back as prisoners across the river into Pennsylvania. The area around Trenton provided the scene of one of the decisive victories early in the Revolution.

It was this historic spot that was chosen for the capital after New Jersey had voted to ratify the Constitution, the third state to do so.

PENNSYLVANIA

As we have seen, the land west of the Delaware was inhabited by Quakers. It had been bought from Lord Berkeley by four prominent Quakers, one of whom was William Penn. The purchase of land or its grant by the King left many doubts about boundaries. William Penn wanted to clarify his rights to the colony he had been instrumental in founding. In 1681 he went to England to straighten matters out. It seemed that the Crown owed Penn a debt of about £16,000, a very considerable sum of money. Penn was willing to write off this debt in exchange for a charter to the lands west of the river.

There appears to have been little difficulty about the charter but a considerable problem over the name used to identify it. The charter as prepared left a blank for the name. Penn wanted to name it New Wales, because the lands were said to be hilly like Wales, but the King's secretary refused to enter this name. Penn then made another suggestion, that it would be named Sylvania, a Latin form meaning "wooded." The secretary took this name to the King, who made a change knowing that, as a Quaker, Penn would not want a name honoring a person, even the King himself. In what he evidently considered a joke, the King called the land Pennsylvania.

No amount of effort on Penn's part could get this changed, so Pennsylvania it remained. The King tried to make him feel better about the matter by saying it was really in honor of Penn's father, an admiral. But Penn's scruples had been outraged and his pleasure in the new grant of land was a little soured.

Penn came to his new lands the next year. His attitude toward the Indians was always kind and strictly fair. Almost his first act upon arriving was to meet with the chiefs of the various Indian tribes to arrange a treaty of "purchase and amity." He did not feel he had the right to appropriate their lands, he wanted to buy them. That same year he prepared and presented to the colonists his "Frame of Government." This was Pennsylvania's first written constitution. The heart of his theory — which was unusual in 1682 — was "any government is free to the people under it [whatever the frame] where the laws rule, and the people are a party to those laws."

William Penn planned this to be a great province and he wanted to found a city that would be worthy to be its capital. There was already a sizable community along the river which was also a seaport and this he took to be his capital city. There are many possibilities to choose from as to his source of the name but the one that seems most probable is that it came from a sentence that St. Paul wrote to the Romans: "Be kindly affectionate one to another with brotherly love." But in the Greek in which St. Paul wrote, the word meaning "brotherly love" was *philadelpheia*. Penn used it in the Latin form when he chose Philadelphia.

Philadelphia was not only the major city, seaport and the

capital of the colony — it was also the seat of the federal government. Nearly one hundred years after Penn made it the capital of his grant it served for repeated assemblies of the Continental Congress and of the Congress of the United States. It was even considered as a possible choice for the capital of the nation.

Philadelphia was patriotic from the beginning. It was the home of the Declaration of Independence and the seat of the meetings which produced our Constitution. The state, founded by Quakers, was the second to ratify the work for freedom done in its capital city.

Philadelphia did not remain the capital of the state for very long after the United States came into being. The new capital was named Lancaster, after the county in England, although it had first been called Hickory Town when it was laid out in 1730. In 1812 they moved the new capital a little farther west to the town of Harrisburg.

A ferry had been opened across the Susquehanna River about 1712 and a village grew up around it which gradually began to be called by the name of the man who owned the ferry. Harrisburg was the form the name took. The story goes that this man's son believed that his town would some day be the capital of the Commonwealth of Pennsylvania. He even laid out a tract of land "to be held in trust until the legislature sees fit to use it." In 1812 his foresight was rewarded and the town named for his father and himself became the capital city of the great state of Pennsylvania.

There are various reasons given why Pennsylvania has been nicknamed "The Keystone State." One suggestion is that it was so named because there were six colonies to the north and six colonies to the south of it, which made it the keystone of the arch of the thirteen new states. But over the years Pennsylvania has been a keystone state in more ways than one.

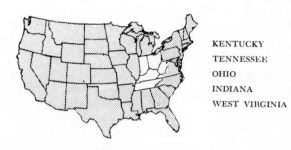

KENTUCKY
TENNESSEE
OHIO
INDIANA
WEST VIRGINIA

6. Westward Ho!

The Thirteen Colonies which made up the original thirteen states all lay along the Atlantic seaboard. The time had come for Americans to spread out across the country.

The Revolution had ended and there was peace in the land. As far west as the Mississippi there were new areas open to the sons and grandsons of those who had founded the colonies, built the cities, fought for freedom and established a government. The people no longer thought of themselves as English (or Dutch or French or German) but as Americans. The new areas provided the opportunity for the next wave of pioneers and for the flow of Americans westward in a movement that was, in the next hundred years, to clear the land to the Pacific Ocean.

From Virginia, the people pushed across the mountains into what was to become Kentucky. North Carolina extended its borders to include what we know as Tennessee. From Pennsylvania, where the mountains had already been crossed, the pioneers moved down into the western part of Virginia. This region was later to cut itself off from the mother state and become West Virginia. And Daniel Boone led the movement westward.

72

KENTUCKY

Daniel Boone was not the first white man who had traversed the wilderness west of the mountains, but he was by all odds the most famous. Boone has become a true American hero. Picture him with his buckskin jacket, his coonskin cap and his long rifle. Leaving the farm near Reading, Pennsylvania, where he was born, he was hired, in 1769, to explore the forests and fields and streams of what was even then known as Kentucky. He was to open up what came to be called the Wilderness Road.

Daniel Boone had many adventures. While we cannot believe *all* the stories told of him, no doubt many are true. Without his work the development of the country west of Pennyslvania might have been delayed. Before his death Congress, at the instigation of the Kentucky legislature, praised the pioneer who had "opened the way to millions of his fellow men."

This intrepid woodsman led a small band of men into the wilderness. Brought up in areas which were mountainous or heavily wooded, they were surprised at the open lands they found. (These meadows we now call "blue grass country.") "Very clear," one of them wrote, "not a bush on it. I could see the buffaloes in it two miles off."

This was Kentucky. The name, with this exact spelling, was recorded by a Major Trent fifteen years before Boone's appearance there. Some people say that it means "dark and bloody ground." Others think that it comes from an Indian word "kenta-ke" which means a plain or meadowland, a more accurate description. The State of Virginia had a vague claim upon the area, having established it as a county about the time of the Revolution, using the already well-known name.

In less than twenty-five years after Boone and his companions ventured into the wilderness, settlers had followed them in such numbers that the state was admitted to the Union in 1792. There was no question under what name it would come in. Kentucky led the way for all the new states in the West.

There is a story told about the origin of the name of the capital city of Kentucky which illustrates the dangers faced by those who went into the wilderness. Details of the story may have been added as time went by, but there was evidently a group of men on their way westward to a "salt lick" which they proposed to work. One evening they camped by a ford in the Kentucky River. During the night they were attacked by Indians and one of their number, a man named Stephen Frank, was killed. In time a town grew up around the ford and its name naturally became "Frank's Ford" and eventually was changed to Frankfort. This town was chosen as the capital at the time that the state was admitted to the Union.

Although many of Boone's exploits have been exaggerated by the passage of time, the State of Kentucky did not forget his contribution. Twenty-five years after his death his remains, along with those of his wife, were brought back to Frankfort where a monument to him was erected.

TENNESSEE

Some people say that Daniel Boone discovered Tennessee. Probably others had been there before him but Boone's name is linked with the whole area. His reputation probably influenced settlers to move into the new land. The man who really led the newcomers into the territory, however, was James Robertson. Only a few years after Boone went into Kentucky the pioneers moved westward beyond the earlier boundaries of North Carolina. They found themselves in Cherokee country. One of the important Indian towns bore a name they themselves did not know the meaning of. It had been recorded as early as 1717 by an Englishman who wrote this name as "Tinnase," which is certainly simpler than the form we later gave it. The very large river, at first called just the Cherokee River, later took its name from the Cherokee town and was called the Tennessee River. By the outbreak of the Revolution several valleys were dotted with peaceful homesteads.

In 1777, North Carolina organized its western lands as a county, calling it Washington. The next year a settlement near the present site of Nashville attempted to set up a separate government, calling itself the State of Franklin. Three years later, North Carolina abandoned the idea of controlling this tract. It was ceded to the United States Government and was named the Territory South of the Ohio River, but everyone kept right on calling it the "Tennessee Country."

With only about 35,000 people, it was the least populous of any state when, in 1796, a constitutional convention met as a preliminary to statehood. Tradition has it that a young man named Andrew Jackson, who became the first President from the new lands to the west, proposed that the name of the new state should be Tennessee. There does not appear to have been much argument about it. So the third new state was admitted, but it would be hard to say whether it was named for a Cherokee town, the river, or the woods and mountains and meadows that had taken the name as their own so long before.

Its other name, its nickname, did not come to it for many years. When the governor called for volunteers to serve in the Mexican War in 1847, such an unprecedented number came forward that it has used the name ever since — "The Volunteer State."

Knoxville was named the capital city. A few years later a chain of fortifications was built on a great bend in the Cumberland River. The name of Nashborough was used, in honor of General Francis Nash, a hero of the Revolution. As a town grew up on the other side of the river it also used the name Nashborough until the citizens decided that this sounded too British and they changed the name to Nashville.

The highest land in the town was a hill called Cedar Knob. The owner, who evidently did not believe in long-term real estate investment, sold the hill in 1811 for one cow. Thirty years later, when the state legislature decided to make Nashville the capital, they built the new capitol building on the still beautiful hill of Cedar Knob.

OHIO

Just as Tennessee lies to the south of Daniel Boone's Kentucky, so to the north of it lies Ohio. The State of Ohio owes its name first to the Indians and then to the French. In the course of the French explorations, they recorded the name of a great river flowing into the Mississippi, using the

Iroquois name for it. This meant "road" (or sometimes river) with the *io* giving the added meaning of "fine." This river was the Ohio, and a fine river it was. Its name had been in use since the days of Sieur Robert Cavalier de La Salle, the French explorer whose adventures we shall read about in another chapter.

A number of Indian tribes lived beside the long river. Each tribe named its own part in its own tongue. In the eastern part it was called "Olighin" in the Algonquin language. A Moravian missionary wrote of it as "The Ohio, as it is called by the Senecas. Allegheny is the name of the same river in the Delaware language. Both names signify fine or fair river." So today the Allegheny River starts in the extreme northern part of Pennsylvania and meanders its way to Pittsburgh, where it is joined by the Monongahela. A little west of there the Allegheny changes its name to the Ohio. It runs southwest, forming the southern boundaries of Ohio, Indiana and Illinois, flowing into the Mississippi at Cairo, Illinois.

The land came to be known by the name of the river. Virginia confirmed this name when it designated the area as Ohio County during the Revolution. The government, by treaty with the British, acquired the land east of the Mississippi. All that land north of the Ohio and west of the Alleghenies was combined into what was called the "Northwest Territory."

People came in great numbers to the rich fields and pleasant valleys. Many of the newcomers migrated from Connecticut to settle on land bordering Lake Erie which that state had retained when its claims to the western areas were ceded to the United States. This was called the Western Reserve. It retains many of its New England characteristics even today. Men from Massachusetts, too, bought up land and began to build the town of Marietta on the shore of the Ohio River. In fact, Ohio was becoming populated before George Washington took the oath of office.

Ohio was a part of various territories until 1799 when its own territory was established. The first seat of the territorial government was at Marietta.

Ohio was the first state of the Northwest Territory to be admitted to the Union. This was in 1803. Naturally, it came in under the Indian name meaning "fine river" which had been written down by the French explorers more than a hundred years before.

Ohio did not wait long before establishing a state capital. They went at it in a business-like way, the state asking every community what they would offer in order to get the capital to settle in its town. The town promoters of Franklin-town, on the banks of the Scioto River, made such a good offer and had such a beautiful location that their bid was accepted in 1812. As the name of the town commemorated Benjamin Franklin this might have seemed satisfactory. However, the legislature decided to go even further back and chose the name Columbus. Perhaps they, too, felt that they had found a beautiful new world.

There is a legend that the state got its nickname from an Indian exclamation at the sight of a very tall man. The Indian is reported to have shouted "Hetalk!" This meant "big buckeye." It seems more probable, however, that the name derives from the large number of buckeye trees in the state. These are related to the horse chestnut of Europe and the seeds of both trees are similar.

INDIANA

Ohio's next neighbor to the west — the state we call Indiana — was almost wholly owned and occupied by Indians, although white men, largely traders, had been in and out of it since the late 1600's. The French brought eight families in to form a permanent settlement in 1735 at the place which they, and we, call Vincennes. About fifty years after the French came to this settlement the entire territory passed under American control.

It took longer to take care of the Indians. There was an unceasing effort to drive them out. The Indian wars were endless.

The last particularly difficult Indian chief was called Little Turtle. He had defeated the two expeditions which Washington had sent in to subdue him. Finally General Anthony Wayne took over and, after training his men for months in Indian tactics, they successfully avoided an ambush set up by Little Turtle and completely defeated his force.

Twenty years before the first American settlers moved in, a company calling itself the Indiana Company had been formed for the purpose of what we should now term "dealing in real estate." Its sponsors were engaged in rather dubious deals on the east bank of the Ohio, not far from Pittsburgh. Although defeated by the State of Virginia, which challenged its claims to the territory, the Indiana Company became known to the public. Its name was revived when the Indiana Territory was separated from the Northwest Territory in 1800. Indiana was granted statehood in 1816.

Some authorities contend that the name was chosen because the territory had so many Indians. Only the added letter "a" changed it from Indian Territory. But it is hard to understand why the inhabitants would take over a somewhat discredited name, originally applied to land not even in the state, and which reminded them of the Indians with whom they had had such bitter struggles.

Once statehood had been obtained they had to choose a capital city. The commission set up to choose the site and the name decided on a small village in almost the exact center of the new state. Even then, it seemed, they could not get away from the Indians. They took the name of their state and added the Greek word *polis,* meaning city, arriving at the name Indianapolis, in much the same way that Maryland had done with Annapolis more than a hundred years earlier.

The word Hoosier is well known as applied to the state and its inhabitants. Its derivation is not clear, but it is one of the best-known state nicknames we have: we have Hoosier poets, Hoosier football teams, and just plain Hoosiers.

WEST VIRGINIA

West Virginia, despite its name, is more like its neighbors Pennsylvania, Kentucky and Tennessee than it is like its parent State of Virginia.

It has been said that the biggest British blunder, one

which led at least indirectly to the Revolution, was the Proclamation of 1763 which prohibited settlement beyond the crest of the Alleghenies. Americans resented being limited as to where they could go! It angered them that any barrier should be imposed against their taking land and holding it for themselves if they were strong enough to do so.

Yet the Alleghenies curve southwest from east-central Pennsylvania along the entire western boundary of Virginia, effectively cutting off movement of immigration from east to west. Only from western Pennsylvania could there be movement into what is now West Virginia. Indeed, most of its settlers did not come from Virginia at all, but from Pennsylvania. The immigrants were men hungry for land. It was the Scotch-Irish squatters of western Pennsylvania who complained to the British governor that it was "against the laws of God and Nature, that so much land should be idle while so many Christians wanted it to labor on."

Because of the difficulty of crossing the mountains it was the adventurers, the frontiersmen, the "Daniel Boones," who made the western part of Virginia so different from the "Old Dominion," which had been founded more than a century earlier. There was more than a measure of time between them, more than a range of mountains: there was a difference in the people. (The footprints of Daniel Boone led into West Virgina too. He was a prominent citizen in the Kanawha Valley when the population was growing rapidly.)

It was the Civil War which caused this difference to result in the final break. Virginia joined the Confederacy while its western half broke off and sided with the Union.

On June 11, 1861, shortly after Virginia seceded from the

Union, the representatives from the western side of the mountains walked out of Richmond and returned to their own land. There was an overwhelming popular vote in favor of the creation of a new state.

Many people wanted to use the old Indian river name "Kanawha" as the name of the new state. As the western part of the old state was now separate they thought it deserved a new and separate name. But in the end it kept its ties to the old. West Virginia was admitted to the Union in 1863, during the Civil War.

There is a charming tale told about the selection of a city to serve as the capital. Just before the Revolution, a settlement was founded by a Colonel George Clendenin which he named after his father, calling it Charles Town. This was one of two cities being given consideration. Two representatives from Charles Town were touring the state trying to get people to vote for their selection of the capital but they met with little interest from most of the populace. Despairing at the short time remaining for them to make any progress, they told their tale to a stranger in the hotel. The stranger turned out to be Lowlow, a noted circus clown. For the remaining days before voting time he stopped the performance at a given point and allowed five minutes for the representatives of Charleston, as the city was now called, to plead for the votes of the audience.

At the succeeding election everyone who had attended the circus must have voted for Charleston for there was no question of its selection.

The state's informal name "The Mountain State" is most appropriate. Its eastern and southern sections are filled with mountains and only in the northwest section does it begin to flatten out as the land nears the Ohio River.

The names of English kings, queens and aristocrats had been left behind along the seacoast. The ties with England had given way before the onset of Americanism. Three out of the four first Western states to come into the Union had names of Indian origin and the fourth — Indiana — simply chose a different approach to an Indian name. Three of the four, too, were the names of rivers, a custom that had been started by Connecticut and Delaware but which was to continue as the pioneers moved on westward. As we shall see, calling the state after a large river seems to be a part of our naming pattern.

FLORIDA
TEXAS
CALIFORNIA
NEVADA
COLORADO
OKLAHOMA
UTAH
NEW MEXICO
ARIZONA

7. *The Spanish Cavaliers*

The Spanish were the earliest explorers of the southern part of the North American continent. They followed closely on the discoveries of Columbus and the development of the West Indies, as we came to call them. The year 1513 marked the beginning of their explorations of the mainland. In that year Balboa, led by Indians, crossed the narrow strip of land that connected North and South America. On its far side he stood astounded on the shore: he was the first white man to view the Pacific Ocean. He knelt and thanked "God and all the Heavenly Host who had reserved the prize of so great a thing unto him, being a man but of small wit and knowledge, of little experience and lowly parentage." Balboa fully realized his good fortune.

In the same year another important move toward the West was made. Juan Ponce de León, the Governor of Puerto Rico, set sail from that island with three ships. His purpose was "to win honor and increase estate." It was also, so the books tell us, to discover the fountain of youth.

Only six days after Easter Sunday, which in Spanish is called the Easter of Flowers, they sighted an unknown island. As Herrera the Chronicler wrote the story, they called the land Florída, both for the Easter of Flowers and the green and flowery appearance of the land. (When the English came they changed the pronunciation to Flórida.) This name, given in the year 1513, was the first place name on the North American continent to be spoken by white men who came from overseas. It has lasted for nearly four hundred and fifty years.

But Ponce sailed back still believing he had named a new island. In giving a name to the new land he was following the King's instructions to all his captains: "Arrived there by good providence. First of all you must give a name to the country, as a whole, and to the cities, towns, and places," or again, "First you must name all the cities, towns, and places which you find there."

It was customary for those discoverers of new lands to give their own names to the rivers, capes, and other places; often they used the name of a saint on whose day they made the discovery or one with whom they felt a close connection. Common also were those names which, like the names given by the Indians, were at first merely descriptions like pilot's memoranda, such as Canebrake Cape, which came to us as Cape Canaveral. They also used some incident: thus at a little island Juan Ponce's men took 170 turtles and so called it Tortugas, a name which still survives.

There were other Spaniards who followed Ponce to the new mainland. The first islands which Columbus had discovered had been left behind: Haiti and the large island of Cuba were already filled with the Spanish less than twenty years after his ships the *Nina,* the *Pinta* and the *Santa Maria* had first sighted their landfall. All the rich and adventurous Spaniards were anxious to gain possession of the unexplored continent to the West. Most of them had heard tales of the rich countries which were filled with gold and precious jewels.

Hernándo Cortéz, a wealthy and powerful Spaniard, determined to conquer this land and win its riches. In 1519 he sailed to perform this mission. He took with him nearly 600 Spaniards, 200 Indians and 16 horses. When he reached the port of Vera Cruz on the coast of Mexico he burned his ships to show his men his determination to stay there and to conquer the country. He was, of course, attacking a large Indian nation. He might never have succeeded if the people had been united or if he had not been taken by some of them for a Mexican hero, Quetzalcoatl, who, tradition said, would come back to bless them. But Cortéz was a determined man and his firearms, armor and horses gave him an advantage.

Forcing his way across the peninsula to the Aztec city of Mexico, he captured the Mexican ruler. After more than two years of fighting he and his little army were the masters of Mexico.

Other Spaniards followed him. De Soto crossed the whole southern part of what is now the United States, but he gave his life to the adventure and only a few of his followers escaped to the coast of Mexico. Coronado set out from Mexico in 1540 with eleven hundred men. He, too, was in search of treasure but he was destined not to find much of it. However, he explored the whole area of what is now the southwestern section of the United States; from the southern part of California he worked his way east through New Mexico as far as the borders of Oklahoma.

As time went on, more and more Spaniards ventured to the north and the Spanish rule expanded. Sometimes they were in conflict with the French, later with the Americans, but over the years the Spanish dominated the whole Southwest. For three hundred years they held on, then the Mexicans threw off Spanish rule and created the Federal Republic of Mexico which then controlled a region roughly corresponding in size to Texas, New Mexico, Arizona, Utah, Nevada, and California.

The Spanish in Mexico had got along well with the Indians. They had been good settlers and colonizers. They had built up an empire in the new lands. But the United States was pressing them throughout their northern territories.

The men in Texas revolted against Mexico and won their freedom a few years after the Mexicans had won theirs from Spain. The United States considered that the boundary was the Rio Grande but the Mexicans never acknowledged it. When United States forces moved to the river the Mexicans pushed them back and the Mexican War began on May 12, 1846.

In the course of this war the United States Army under General Scott landed at Vera Cruz and eventually took the capital city where they raised their flag over the "Halls of the Montezumas." General Zachary Taylor gained the northern provinces of Mexico and Colonel Kearny captured New Mexico. When he moved on to take California, which at that time included not only the strip along the coast as we now know it but extended far inland, a squadron of the United States Navy, helped by American settlers, had already raised the flag over the province.

The Mexicans finally capitulated and a treaty was signed in 1848. It gave us the boundary of the Rio Grande and from El Paso went in an almost straight line to the Pacific. We also paid the Mexicans $15 million and took over some of their obligations to American citizens.

Out of these Mexican lands came six of our great states including Texas, which had won her own fight earlier.

FLORIDA

When Juan Ponce de León first landed on the shores of the mainland, he did not know what he had accomplished. He had set out to discover "Bimini," a fabulous island. What he came to was the coast of the peninsula which became our Florida. Juan, however, explored both coasts and was convinced that he had discovered a huge island. He reported this to the King, who gave him a grant to colonize "the island of Bimini and the island of Florida." However, Juan's reign as governor did not last long. Disease and an Indian arrow ended his career. His famous "Fountain of Youth" had turned out to be of little help to him.

The French Huguenots came in a little later and made attempts at a settlement which did not succeed. The French occupation was broken by the Spanish in a large sea battle off the Florida shore. Florida, many years later, was still claimed by the Spanish to extend much farther north than it does now. Spain also claimed and held for many years the Sea Islands along the entire southern coastline of South Carolina. But the British were winning everywhere on the North American continent. In 1763, at the close of the war with France, in which Spain had joined, all the land from

Florida to the Mississippi was ceded to England. The British made good progress in colonization but they held the land for only twenty years when, by another treaty after the American Revolution, it was returned to Spain.

Eventually the western portion, called West Florida, came into the possession of the United States although this was still disputed by the Spanish. Finally, in 1819, Spain formally ceded all its holdings in the southeast to the United States, but this, in a way, only confirmed what the Americans had already taken over.

During its troubled history Spain never entirely succeeded in colonizing Florida. The various occupations of France, Britain, and the pressures of the United States had kept it unsettled and had hindered development. Even after acquiring this tract the United States did not establish civil government there for several years. The new Territory of Florida had to wait until 1845 to become a state of the American Union.

Despite its varied ownership, its changes of status and its constant trouble with the Indians, the new territory and subsequently the state were accepted under the old name given by a Spaniard nearly 350 years before.

When the new territory was established the United States chose for the capital an attractive location on a hill several hundred feet above sea level, surrounded by rolling hills, lakes and streams and shaded by giant trees. It is not, however, anywhere near the center of the state, being nearly four hundred miles from the tip of the peninsula. It is told that the Spaniards fortified a hill near the site when warring with the Indians and subsequently made a settle-

ment there. The state kept the old Indian name Tallahassee
and this was retained when the state came into the Union.

Florida is credited with a number of nicknames, each in
its way descriptive of the state. The vast swamps in its
southern part, called the Everglades, are unique. One name
it is popularly known by is the "Everglade State." But it is
also called the "Sunshine State" as winter visitors from all
over the Midwest and the East can readily accept.

TEXAS

It was inevitable that the Spanish in Mexico should look
longingly at the lands to the north of them but they did very
little to settle them.

The Spaniards, like the French, were in the habit of
claiming everything in sight. So they claimed that part of
the Gulf coast north of Mexico and of the Rio Grande. Here
there was a tribe of Indians called Teyas. At one time an
expedition arrived at an Indian town. The townspeople
hailed it with the words "Teysha!" This was supposed to
mean "Hello, friends!" So this name was given to this country. The name was spelled Texias, Tejas, Tejias, Techan,
but finally Texas.

So the area had a name, but even as late as 1829, when
Mexico revolted from Spanish rule, there were only about
four thousand Europeans in Texas, but there were multitudes
of Indians. In order to open up the country the Mexicans began to encourage Americans to come and settle. Once the
country was free to them Americans began arriving in
large numbers. After a time the Mexicans repented of their
offer but the Americans kept coming in anyway. Later the

Mexicans must have been even sorrier they had permitted this because it was the Americans who took away their province.

Two of the famous men of early Texas came there at that time: one was Stephen Austin, who led the first colony of five thousand Americans into the province. The other man was General Sam Houston who commanded the Texas forces which won independence.

In 1835 the Texans realized that they could escape from domination by the Mexicans only through fighting for their freedom. Almost to a man they rose up and in two and a half months drove all the Mexicans south of the Rio Grande. Then they set up arrangements for their own government and prepared to meet the Mexicans who returned under General Santa Anna to crush the revolution. The Mexicans might have succeeded except for the bravery of 183 men. They held the old fort of the Alamo, which was under siege by large forces, for thirteen days. Only six men were alive when the besiegers overran the fort and these were massacred.

Their sacrifice had not been in vain, for "Remember the Alamo" became a cry not only to the Texans but to the people of the United States. Boatloads of volunteers sailed to help their beleaguered friends. Mexico tried to stop their coming and the United States issued orders telling them not to go, but the American sympathizers could not be stopped. Since they declared themselves to be colonists seeking homes in Texas, there was no way to stop them from offering their lives after they got there.

Then came the decisive battle after months of falling

back discouraged. At the battle of San Jacinto, under the command of General Sam Houston, the Mexican forces were routed. Their leader Santa Anna was captured and a treaty was finally signed by the officers in the field. This provided that the Mexicans would withdraw from Texas below the Rio Grande. Although the State of Mexico was too busy with its other troubles to ratify the treaty, the Americans went on setting up their own independent republic; they adopted their own consitution and designed their own flag. This was one five-pointed star on a vertical blue field with two horizontal bars of red and of white and gave rise to the nickname the state has always borne — "The Lone Star State."

Texas was recognized as an independent republic by the United States and several European nations, but Texans really wanted to become part of the United States. The possibility of doing so was all bound up with the question of its wanting to remain a slave-owning state. Many Northern members of Congress objected to this. However, in 1845 Texas became the twenty-eighth state of the Union, under the old Indian greeting of Techas, then spelled Texas.

Texans have been noted since the beginning for their independence, their brave fighters, their generosity and hospitality. No wonder the motto of the state is "Friendship." They showed their independence when they came to decide upon their capital city. Instead of picking a city already in existence — San Antonio or Galveston might have served — they went up into the middle of the state and picked a spot in the wilderness. It was a pleasing spot but they had to start from scratch. They named it Austin in honor of the man who had brought in so many Americans and who had once gone to prison in Mexico City for upholding the rights of the Americans.

Years later an American humorist, Irvin S. Cobb, visited Texas and reported that he had found "a timbered tract as large as Massachusetts, a cotton patch in the Black Waxy country as big as all Ohio, a grazing belt in the Panhandle as large as Pennsylvania, more wheatlands than in either of the Dakotas, and more corn fields than Illinois." His statement is fairly accurate but he overlooked the rich mining country and the oil fields dotted with derricks.

CALIFORNIA

One of the captains of Cortéz, the conqueror of Mexico, heard a tale from the Indians which he took back to Cortéz. He told the tale of a strange island, rich in jewels and gold, inhabited only by women. Men were allowed to come only on visits.

The similarity of this description to a popular romance called *The Deeds of Esplandian* undoubtedly struck Cortéz. The story had been widely read and no doubt Cortéz knew of it. In the story there was such an island, near the Indies. The queen of that island was named Calafia. Cortéz himself, according to his historian, coined the name California, saying that must be the name of the island the Indians were talking about.

When, a few years later, Cortéz himself sailed westward, he came to what he took to be this island. But there were no jewels, no gold, and no beautiful women. Since he did not sail all around the land, he departed in the belief that he had, indeed, found the island but had been misled about what would be there. Instead, he had explored the tip of a long peninsula which we now call Lower California. This remains a part of Mexico to this day.

The Mexicans, however, were not satisfied to let things rest and the name was gradually applied to all the land along the west coast and for hundreds of miles inland. Explorers sailed past and may have penetrated the area along the coast. Sir Francis Drake repaired his ships in Drake's Bay; Sebastian Vizcaíno discovered the Bay of Monterey about 1600; but for 150 years thereafter there was little additional knowledge of the land. During most of this period California was believed to be an island or a group of islands. Not until 1769 did anyone even find the body of water which we now know as San Francisco Bay.

The missionaries really took California for the Spanish. There were many missions established, beginning as early as the end of the seventeenth century. Perhaps little progress was made in educating or civilizing the Indians, whom they treated almost as slaves on their great properties, but they did a great deal to develop the land for profitable crops and large herds of cattle. The country was nevertheless under strict military and political rule from Mexico. Foreigners were not welcome but they began to come in anyway: Russians from the north, the Hudson's Bay Company from Canada, as well as American hunters and trappers. Overland migration from the United States began only about 1840. Although there is said to have been merely seven hundred American residents in northern California in 1845, there was already talk of getting the area to secede from Mexico.

At that time Captain J. C. Frémont appeared on the scene, an American on a government surveying expedition. Practically on his own he undertook to separate California from Mexico. There was a show of force on both sides. Frémont caused a band of Mexican cavalry mounts to be seized and persuaded some American settlers to occupy Sonoma in the northern part. There was talk about making California an independent republic. A flag was designed for it. This flag, with a bear as an emblem, flew for a few days over Sonoma. Fortunately, this incident was quickly merged in the larger situation, for the Mexican War had started on the Rio Grande. The flag of the United States was raised over Monterey, proclaiming that California was a part of the United States. A year or two later, at the end of the war, Mexico ceded California (called by the Mexicans Alta California in contrast to the peninsula called Baja California, which Mexico retained) to the United States, thus making everything legal. On September 9, 1850, California was admitted to the Union as the thirty-first state.

In the meantime gold had been discovered. Americans flocked to California, as many as 80,000 arriving in 1849. Everybody headed for the gold fields. Churches, stores, homes, and offices were deserted. Soldiers left their ships in the harbor. It is said that at one time five hundred ships were idle in the bay because the sailors had scooted off to the foothills. Soon there were half a million people in the state and California was off on its fabulous boom. People who had been poor all their lives became millionaires. The prospector who made a good strike may have had moderate or unbelievable gains; the unlucky ones probably died in a ditch. The excitement was so great that even becoming a state — named for a fictional queen on a mythical island by a Spanish grandee nearly 350 years before — must have been something of an anticlimax. The gold rush even carried over to the state's nickname. It is not called "El Dorado" or "The Golden State" for nothing.

Long before this the Californians had explored a little to the east from the head of the San Francisco Bay along two rivers, one of which they had named San Joaquin for the saint who, tradition said, was the father of the Virgin. The other they named Sacramento for the Holy Sacrament. Soon after 1800 a wealthy Swiss named John A. Sutter arrived in California and was given a grant of land of fifty thousand acres beside the Sacramento River. He built himself a castle and a fort bristling with cannon. He became the center of American activities in the Mexican province where he lived in state in his castle. As more Americans came he laid out a town along the river which was named Sacramento.

This was the river that made it possible to link the Pacific Ocean with the Missouri River. Ships could leave St. Louis and arrive at Sacramento by following the rivers for two thousand miles or more. Here the steamers from San Francisco brought supplies for the northern gold miners. It took a Pony Express rider eight days to reach this point with the news of Lincoln's assassination, and to this point came the overland stages, through mud and dirt, all the way from St. Joseph on the western border of Missouri.

Sacramento was the town which was chosen as the new capital of the new state. John Sutter had died in poverty, his fort was no longer useful, his herds were dispersed, but his town went on to fame as the center of a great state which had been built on Spanish rule, missions, Indians, enterprising Americans, sea and river traffic, and gold. It has never quite forgotten this.

NEVADA

Nevada seems to have had a hard time becoming a state. Nevada had never been a local name and so there was no history connected with it.

The area we call Nevada had been a part of California. This had belonged to Mexico until the end of the Mexican War in 1848. Then Mexico handed over the lands she still had north and west of the Rio Grande to the United States. When California achieved statehood in 1850 all the area to the east was given to Utah which was then organized as a territory. But the western part of this area was a long way from the seat of territorial government in Utah and got very little protection. The people in this western section made their first try then at getting some self-government. Utah replied with a gesture by turning its western part into the county of Carson, named for Kit Carson.

Since the city of Carson was laid out shortly afterward and became the capital when the state was admitted, let us have a look at Kit Carson. One might say that he was the Daniel Boone of the West. By the time he was seventeen he was a professional hunter, a renowned trapper, and an expert guide through the wildernesses of the Western states. He went with John C. Frémont on his explorations and was with him on the famous California expedition when Frémont almost succeeded in making an independent republic of the state. Carson served in the Mexican War and was rewarded with the title of brigadier-general for "important services in New Mexico, Arizona and Indian Territory." Like Boone, there are more stories told of him than can possibly be true. But that he was a famous Indian fighter and a brave resourceful man cannot be questioned.

In any case, he was known throughout the West. It was therefore quite fitting that Utah should name a county for him. It was still a wild unsettled land although great numbers of men were passing through on their way to California and its gold.

But Carson County still did not make much progress toward statehood. Congress largely ignored its pleas until in 1859 a rich deposit of silver was discovered high up on the side of a mountain. The Comstock Lode, as it was named, proved to be one of the richest deposits of precious metals. One discovery after another was made. Gold as well as silver attracted hordes of miners. Virginia City, as the mining region was called, became famous the world over.

An effort was again made to achieve statehood in 1863 but it was not granted until the following year. The area had long been called the Washoe country, from the tribe of Indians which inhabited it, and the people wanted the state to be so named. However, Congress did not think this was dignified enough. The Committee on Territories, rather arbitrarily, decided to shorten the name of the mountain range in the state, Sierra Nevada, to Nevada. At least in Washington they decided that the range lay in the new state, but the inhabitants knew better. They were well aware that most of the range lay in California to the west. Nevertheless, no matter how much they wanted Washoe, they were given the name Nevada. In more ways than one the name was unsuitable because Sierra Nevada, meaning a "range of mountains snowed upon," was highly inappropriate since the mountains of the new state got very little snow and not even much rain. But Nevada it became; and Carson City, named for the famous hunter, became the capital.

Perhaps on the whole the name was an improvement over Washoe as the state is very mountainous. Nevada has two suitable nicknames: one is "The Sagebrush State," which is an accurate description of the bush that covers the land; the other is "The Silver State," for the metal on which much of its fame rests.

COLORADO

Colorado had been intermittently explored by the Spanish from the time when Coronado is reported to have entered the area in 1540 until the last records which indicate that the Spanish were there in 1776. For nearly 250 years the Spanish had traveled over the area without settling there permanently. The Spanish claimed much of the area north of the Rio Grande and therefore had some rights to the land which eventually became Colorado. The only imprint they left, however, is the name Colorado which is Spanish.

In 1598 Don Juan de Oñate set out to look for new lands to the north. Moving westward, he and his men came to a great river which the priest who accompanied them wrote down as the Colorado, because its water was almost red. The name persisted because it sounded easy and pleasant on Spanish tongues.

American fur traders began to come into the mountainous area after the American Revolution but it was not until the Louisiana Purchase, which gave the eastern part of the state to the United States, that surveys were begun to find out what we had really acquired. Since it relates to the French, the Louisiana Purchase is described in the next chapter. In 1806 the far-ranging explorer, Zebulon Pike, was surveying for the government in the new land of Louisiana. He followed the Arkansas River into Colorado and probably was the first civilized man to see the 14,000-foot-high peak which came to be known by his name, although he himself had originally called it Grand Peak. It is, of course, only one of about fifty peaks in Colorado that are just as high, but lying so near the eastern plains and standing practically alone, Pikes Peak is undoubtedly the best known and perhaps the most impressive.

In 1858 gold was discovered on the plains near Denver, but no one except Pike, Major Long who followed him, and the fur traders knew much about Colorado. There additional discoveries were made in the mountains and the gold rush was on. A flood of settlers followed. Prospectors studied the likely sites for gold and silver. Semiprecious stones were found and great wealth from coal mining. The minerals and the precious metals really populated the state. Within three years of the first rush of prospectors the area was made a territory.

The problem seems to have been what the place should be called. Rarely had there been such argument in Congress, much of it quite uninformed as to the real status of the area they were talking about. Who had ever heard of a land with so many mountains? One name after another was considered: Colona Territory, Lafayette, Jefferson, Franklin, Columbus, Idaho, Yampe, San Juan, Lulu, Arapaho, and so on until the poor Senators hardly knew what land they were talking about.

However, the delegate from the proposed territory clung to the name Colorado. Finally, 263 years after Oñate had named the river Colorado, the territory was granted the name. Statehood was conferred in 1876. They could have named it "Centennial," for it became a state just a hundred years after the Declaration of Independence. But the word did become the state's nickname.

However, there were still difficulties. When surveys were completed it was found that the Colorado did not flow anywhere within the boundaries of the state. The local legislators were not daunted. They noted that the Grand River, eastern branch of the Colorado, rose in the mountains west of Denver. They therefore passed an act saying: "The name of the Grand River in Colorado is hereby changed to the Colorado River." In this way, Colorado brought its name river back into its own boundaries.

The name of the man to whom the State of Colorado owed so much was chosen as the name of the capital city. James William Denver had had a full career. He had organized a company of infantry and led it across Mexico in the Mexican War. Two years later he was in the California gold fields. He killed a man in a duel the same year he was elected to Congress. Yet when the relations between Kansas and its western part (for all of Colorado was originally a part of Kansas Territory) were growing difficult, the President sent James Denver to settle things. A party of miners named their settlement Denver and it became the capital of the new state.

OKLAHOMA

For years the United States Government had been trying to find out what to do with the Indians who were being displaced by the white settlers. Many Indian wars, with terrible deeds on both sides, took place because the Indians wanted to stay on their own lands and the settlers wanted the land for themselves.

Indians from the East had been moved into eastern Kansas before the middle of the nineteenth century. The Black Hawk War had driven them from the lower flats of Michigan, across upper Indiana and northern Illinois. The Sioux had given up by treaty nearly thirty million acres in Minnesota. In 1830 Congress offered lands to such eastern Indians as were willing to move beyond the Mississippi. The Indians refused to move and both Georgia and Mississippi began to sell land belonging to the Indians. Finally the Indians had to give in.

So it went across the country. At last, in 1834, Congress established an Indian territory, particularly for the southern Indians, in the fertile valley of the Arkansas River. Each nation that moved in was given its own border, could have its own council and make its own laws. A large part of this

Indian territory was left unoccupied for the benefit of north-western Indians who might later be put there. Over the years many other tribes were moved in.

Still the Americans pressed for more land. Finally the government bought land from the Cherokees and Seminoles and, taking the hitherto unassigned land, set aside a large choice tract in the center of the territory for homesteading by the whites. On April 22, 1889, at least twenty thousand people were on the borders ready to race in and put up the stakes which would mark the corners of their future homes. Mounted soldiers stood guard and no one was supposed to step a foot over the border until the bugle blew at high noon. However, here and there someone sneaked across before the signal, getting in sooner than his neighbor to pick the choicest spots.

No wonder the nickname of the state refers to this exciting though highly unethical practice. It is still sometimes called the "Sooner State."

Over the years more and more territory was opened to the whites. Finally the Indian tribes consented to individual allotments as well as government rule from Washington.

In 1906 Oklahoma and Indian territories qualified for statehood as one state under the name Oklahoma, and a year later this was accomplished.

It was a new state with an old name. And although the Americans now owned most of the property and made most of the laws, the name was Indian. Forty years before, at the time when a treaty was being made with one of the Indian tribes, the Commissioner of Indian Affairs asked the delegates, "What would you call your territory?" The leader of the delegation, an educated Choctaw chief, immediately replied, "Oklahoma." The name which he had coined was a simple one in the Choctaw language — *okla,* "people," and *homa,* "red." So the Americans who had displaced the Indians even in their last refuge lived in the "Red People's" state. The name was melodious as was proven seventy-five years later when it became the title of the world's most popular musical comedy.

In fact, when a name for the capital was needed, Oklahoma City was chosen, thus repeating its "Red People's" claim.

UTAH

There were few early explorations of Utah. A Spaniard discovered the Grand Canyon and southern Utah soon after Cortéz captured Mexico. But it took almost 250 years before further explorations were made. From then on it was the fur trappers who opened the territory to future settlers as they did in so many other parts of the West. Men who are part of our heritage made one discovery after another. Jim Bridger first located the Great Salt Lake; Jedediah S. Smith, carrying a rifle in one hand and a Bible in the other, was the first to cross the Salt Lake Desert. John Frémont and Kit Carson explored and mapped the area.

Yet it was the Mormons who founded the state and made it what it is today. But their story did not begin in Utah. It began in 1823 near Palmyra, New York. At that time and place a vision appeared to Joseph Smith. In his vision, Smith said, he saw an American prophet who told him where to find the golden tablets which recorded the stories and prophecies of an ancient race which had lived in the Western Hemisphere about two thousand years before. The followers of Smith reported that he had found the tablets and translated them. This became the *Book of Mormon* upon which the religion of the Latter Day Saints was based.

Smith led his followers from one place to another, always opposed, often with force, by the people among whom they came to live. Their latest resting place, under Smith, was at Nauvoo, Illinois, where they quickly built up a large settlement. But troubles developed and Smith was killed by a mob.

At this point Brigham Young, who took over the leadership, "spoke with the voice of Joseph." Brigham Young became the leader of the Mormons under the magnificent title of "Prophet of the Church of Jesus Christ of the Latter Day Saints." He had read Frémont's reports of the Great Salt Lake Valley and believed that his people should move there.

They had an unbelievable journey. Crossing the Mississippi River on the ice at Nauvoo, they traversed southern Iowa and the length of Nebraska, went up the north bank of the Platte River, crossed to the south bank at Fort Laramie in what is now Wyoming, then jumped the Bear River Divide and the Wasatch Mountains to the valley of the Great Salt Lake. The youthful and the old, with their herds and their household goods, buoyed up by the spirit that moved them, made the incredible journey to their Promised Land.

Brigham Young had a gift for leadership. He is reported to have said that the place he was looking for was the one nobody else wanted. And when he and his band reached Salt Lake Valley he declared, "This is the place."

Here they built schools and temples. They named the place Deseret, a word in the *Book of Mormon* meaning "honey bee."

The "place" was bleak and dried out by the sun so steps were taken to irrigate the land. The first attempt might have been more successful but for a plague of locusts which would certainly have destroyed the crops if the locusts had not been devoured by a flock of birds.

Gradually the desert gave way to trees and gardens. There was no question of the Mormons' progress. They made the lands of their arid country blossom and flourish. They quickly developed vast areas for sheep raising. They opened up extensive mining deposits. They built Salt Lake City as their beautiful capital and as the location of their chief Tabernacle. They were an industrious and a kindly people.

In the treaty with Mexico in 1848 this land was given over to the United States. The next year the Mormons sent a petition to Congress demanding a territorial government. While waiting for this they organized a state of their own under the name of Deseret. A provisional government was set up with Brigham Young as governor. Congress yielded territorial rights but under the name of Utah rather than Deseret which the Mormons wanted. There was an Indian tribe called Yutta by the Spanish. The Americans spelled it Ute or Utah. This name was applied to a lake and a river flowing from it. Many states had been named for their rivers. Congress thought Deseret "sounded too much like desert" and rejected it in favor of Utah but this, too, was not truly acceptable — some of the Indians who went by that name were notoriously lice-infested and dirty, and they ate grasshoppers!

Thus the Territory of Utah came into being, with Fillmore its capital, in honor of the President. Later the capital was changed to Salt Lake City.

Six separate times in a period of nearly forty years efforts were made to have the territory granted statehood. The United States had prohibited polygamy — that is, the right to marry several wives — in several legislative acts between 1862 and 1887, but the Mormon Church held to its right to practice it. In 1890 it capitulated and agreed to give up the practice. Congress then moved and in 1896 the state entered the Union.

There was great celebration in the territory which had waited so long for this. The famous Tabernacle Temple was draped with flags, the largest of them brightly illuminated to show the addition of the forty-fifth star for Utah.

Utah came into the Union a very prosperous state. The Mormons had done wonders with "the place that nobody else wanted." Brigham Young had led his naturally industrious people to security. Since Young had likened their activity to that of a beehive, when he named his land Deseret, the state is nicknamed for that busy insect — "The Beehive State."

NEW MEXICO

This "Land of Enchantment" was explored by the Spaniards in Mexico from the time of their first arrival. Coronado,

Nuño de Guzmán, de Vaca and others, came and left, none the richer for their expeditions. Diego de Ibarra, in 1563, went north and on his return used for the first time the name that lasted. He came back saying he had discovered New Mexico. But others had known this land long before. Man had inhabited the area for possibly fifteen thousand years. We still have ruins of the homes of the cliff-dwelling Indian tribes who lived there over a thousand years ago.

Thirty-five years after Ibarra, Don Juan de Oñate took possession of the lands to the north for King Philip. In an elaborate ceremony he declared that he was claiming "All the realms and provinces of New Mexico." He called the river that he crossed the "river of the north," that is, El Paso del Norte. From this crossing came several names which still remain. The city of El Paso marks the border point between Texas and New Mexico; from that point to the Pacific is the borderline between Mexico and the United States. Oñate wrote that the river "springs and flows from the north and it turns to the east, and there it is called Rio Brave." The Mexicans call the river by that name today but we call its whole length the Rio Grande, meaning simply the "large river."

New Mexico (including Arizona, which was originally a part of it) was ceded to the United States after the Mexican War in 1848. Two years later it was organized as a territory with the land running from the Texas border to that of California. It was still called New Mexico, the same name under which Oñate had claimed it 250 years earlier.

There was opposition in Congress to the name New Mexico. It sounded as though it belonged to Mexico, not to the United States. On the other hand there were those who would rather withdraw from statehood than to change the name.

In spite of this other names were suggested. One of these was Acoma, from an ancient Indian pueblo or town. This name had the advantage of coming before Alabama in the alphabet and would thus head the list of states. This did not seem a very good reason to choose it. Others thought well of the romantic name of Montezuma, the Aztec emperor of Mexico at the time Cortéz arrived there.

New Mexico won out.

But the territory had a long time to wait before it became a state. There was agitation in Congress as to whether it should be a slave or free state. Congress was also dissatisfied with the kind of state constitution that had been suggested. Thirteen years after it became a territory the western half was separated from New Mexico and made a new territory. Land was taken from western Texas and added to New Mexico so that its final boundaries were well established.

Sixty-two years after it had been made a territory and had gone through innumerable changes in form, politics and population, Congress granted it statehood. In spite of all dissension it came into the Union in 1912 under the old, old name of New Mexico.

It had as its capital the town of Sante Fe. This had once been the seat of government of the province of Nueve Mejico when it was called "La Villa Real de la Santa Fe de San Francisco" but which the Indians and the Americans shortened to Santa Fe. Sante Fe is thus the oldest seat of government in the United States. Its altitude is 7,000 feet. The original Spanish plaza is still the heart of the city. On the plaza is the old Governor's Palace, built in 1610. It was here that the Mexican lieutenant governor entertained General Kearny when he marched in with his troops during the Mexican War and it was here, on the Plaza, that General Kearny proclaimed New Mexico to be a part of the United States, and named himself as governor. In a brilliant ceremony he hauled down the Mexican flag and ran up that of the United States.

Probably the day was as brilliantly sunny and clear as it has been in New Mexico most of the time since, so it is no wonder it has been called "The Sunshine State," thus vying with Florida for that distinction. But when its people disliked this competition they called it "Land of Enchantment."

ARIZONA

This state, of course, had the same background and history as New Mexico, of which it was originally a part. It was not long, however, before it was separated from the Territory of New Mexico and in 1863 it was set up separately as the Territory of Arizona.

There is an interesting story about how the name of the territory came to be Arizona. The Spanish were always on the watch for precious metals. About 1730 they heard that great nuggets of silver had been found near a desert spring. The Spaniards took the name from the simple description in the native Indian language. The Indians called it Arishoonak, meaning "little spring." The Spanish fitted it to their own pronunciation and wrote it down as Arizonac or

Arizona. Later a Spanish historian wrote about it under that name but it was not used very much. Then a century later it was revived as the name of a mining company which chose the name Arizona from the old mining district.

When the time came to name the new territory several names were suggested. The one who most stoutly advocated Arizona was a man who was active in the Arizona Mining and Trading Company, who probably saw the advantage to his company. He got it approved both by the Territorial Convention and by Congress.

There is a certain irony in the fact of the territory and later the state being named for a spring that turned out not to have any silver near it at all and that, when the final lines were drawn, also turned out not to be in Arizona but south of it in Mexico. There was still further irony in that the territory had actually been first declared by the Confederate States of America two years before Congress did so. The Confederates' aim to make it a southern state was invalidated by a battalion of California volunteers who soon occupied the region for the Union.

Five weeks after New Mexico was admitted to the Union in 1912, Arizona was also admitted.

Tucson was the first capital, but the permanent capital became a town called Phoenix. A new community had grown up along the lines of the Spanish canal system which some pioneers had rebuilt, making the dry land suitable for ranching. Some student of the classics went back to Ovid, a Roman poet living at the time of Christ, to find a name. Ovid had told of a bird which lived on "frankincense and odoriferous gums. When it has lived five hundred years, it builds itself a nest in the branches of an oak or on top of a palm tree. In this it collects cinnamon, spikenard and myrrh, and of these materials builds a pile on which it deposits itself, and, dying, breathes out its last breath among odors. From the body of the parent bird a young Phoenix issues forth, destined to live as long a life as its parent."

When the community heard the story they enthusiastically adopted the name, assuring themselves, so they may have thought, of a long life for their city. A few years later it was also accepted as the capital.

Geronimo was perhaps the most famous Indian warrior of the Southwest. Not long before the territory was formed his mother, wife and children were killed by the Mexicans. He vowed vengeance on the whites and for years he was the most dreaded Indian in the region. His last series of forays began in 1884 but two years later, hunted down by United States soldiers, he was forced to surrender. He lived on until 1909, a reformed character and a Christian, perhaps in repentance for Mexicans and Americans he had killed.

Arizona has been fortunate in its physical assets. The Grand Canyon is one of the truly great sights in our country and the state has sixteen national monuments and parks besides. Of course its familiar name is "The Grand Canyon State." It has been a rich mining country, highly productive of copper, silver, and gold. Perhaps when the state motto — *Ditat Deus* (God enriches) — was adopted the men who chose the motto were well aware of what they were doing.

LOUISIANA
MISSOURI
MISSISSIPPI
ALABAMA
ARKANSAS
ILLINOIS
MICHIGAN
IOWA
WISCONSIN

8. The French Explorers

Many famous persons helped find and name the rivers and the lands along the Great Lakes, down the Mississippi, up the Missouri, along the Ohio, on to the Gulf.

The English, who opened up the east coast, worked their way westward by land after the Revolution. The French, who first came to the northern part of the continent, had pushed on largely by water.

Jacques Cartier took refuge in a gulf in the year 1534, fifty years before Raleigh sent his people into Virginia. He named it St. Lawrence, for the saint whose name day it was. Then the French pushed on into the gulf and up the mighty river, giving it the same name that Cartier had used.

More than half a century later came Sieur de Champlain, who made many journeys through the lake country below the St. Lawrence River, going almost far enough south to meet Henry Hudson at Albany.

The first permanent French settlement in what we call Canada was made in 1608: Champlain founded Quebec at what he considered a commanding site on the St. Lawrence. This was about the same year that John Smith left Jamestown in Virginia to sail around the bay, the name of which he wrote down as Chisapeake. Sixty years later the French began to look farther west. Louis Joliet is one name connected with these attempts, but before him there had been other Frenchmen exploring the Great Lakes.

No one knows who first called the lakes by their present names. The name for the first lake was taken from the Indians who called it Ontara, to which was added the ending "io," meaning large or beautiful. Next, the French-speaking forest men journeyed by rivers and portages and came to a very large lake which they named for their friends the Hurons who lived there. So we had Lake Huron. Beyond this the explorers went to a still larger lake through the strait they called Sault Ste. Marie. This lake they called Lac Superior, which to the French meant "Upper Lake," but the English later called it only Lake Superior. A superior lake it was, indeed.

Joliet, who had gone to school in France with the Jesuits, but who had been trained in the Canadian woods so that he was at once a priest, an officer of the King and a forest-runner, led his party through a strait out of Lake Huron. (The French word for a strait — a narrow passageway of water leading from one large body of water to another — is *detroit*. Naturally, that was what the French called the passageway between Lake Huron and Lake Erie, little dreaming that the word would turn into the name of a settlement, a town, and in time one of the greatest manufacturing cities in the world: Detroit.) For the lake to which the strait led them they used the name of a friendly tribe of Indians who called themselves Yenish, but the

French shaped the word into something easier to pronounce and named the lake of this tribe Lake Erie.

Then they began to call the fifth of the great lakes they had found Aliniouek or Iliniouek. But the tribe for whom this was named moved farther south, so the lake came to be called merely Michi-guma or Mici-guma, meaning "big water." In the end Michi-guma survived as Lake Michigan and the name Michigan was also applied to the area around it.

In the nearly 150 years since Cartier named the St. Lawrence the French had settled along the bank of that river but had made little progress farther inland. Then, in 1672, the Governor of New France, Comte de Frontenac, appointed Louis Joliet to go on a search for the great river which had been reported by the Indians to be westward. The Governor also appointed Jacques Marquette, a Catholic priest, to go with him.

This river for which they sought was usually called Mis-ispi or Misisipi or by other Indian names sounding somewhat the same. The Indians along the northern reaches of the river used the word "mis" or something like it for "big" and the word "sipi" for "river." Joliet and Marquette, the first Europeans to approach it from the north, carried the name from north to south. We have kept it as Mississippi.

De Soto, a Spaniard, had seen the mouth of the river more than a hundred years before, but his men had called it, in Spanish, the Rio Grande, "big river," which was similar in meaning to the Indian name by which we still know it.

Before Joliet and Marquette got to the "large river" they

had followed the northern shore of Lake Michigan around its bend to the southward. Here they came to a place they called Baie Verte and which the English later called Green Bay. They paddled into a river running westward out of the bay. Farther on they heard of a larger river flowing still more to the west which the Indians called Mescousing or Mesconsing. The name apparently meant "grassy place." The French wrote it down as Ouisconsing, the *oui* being pronounced *w*. Later the English changed the *oui* to *w* but they pronounced it almost the same as the French had — Wisconsin.

Finally they came to the place where this river, known now as the Wisconsin, flowed into the big river they had come so far to see. They had reached the Mississippi! For eight days they drifted down it in their canoes. They did not see a soul. At last they found a path that led to a village where they found some Indians. These were part of the Illinois tribe that had left the northern lake country where their name was first used for the big lake itself.

The root of the name was illini, meaning simply "man." The French had added an *s* to make the word plural and finally it became the even more French-looking word — Illinois — which the French would have called Illin-wa, the *s* being silent. A famous priest wrote, "The word Illinois comes from the Indian Illini, signifying a complete, finished and perfect man, imbued with the spirit and bravery of the men of every nation that ever lived."

So the area and the river both took their names from the tribe.

Still the Frenchmen continued to paddle and float downstream. Then they came upon a wide river pouring in from the northwest. It was so muddy and swift that as it flowed into the Mississippi its course could be traced for miles in the larger stream. So it can today. The Indians called it Pekitanoui, meaning "muddy." Various tribes lived along the river, one of which was called Messouri. We can recognize the *mis* as meaning "big" but no one seems to know whether the rest of the word means "muddy" or "canoes" or something else. Perhaps the Missouri means only "Big Muddy," an accurate but hardly poetic name for so important a river and, as it came to pass, for the land through which it flowed.

The Indians whom the Frenchmen met while exploring around the mouth of the Missouri told of other tribes living up the river. One of these the explorers wrote down as Ouaouiatonon, although what the word sounded like in the Indian tongue is hard to imagine. Nor can one think how Joliet and Marquette pronounced it. In any event, before long they shortened it by dropping the last two syllables. Then they had a strange word made up wholly of vowels — Ouaouia — which must have sounded something like the hoot of an owl.

There are other versions of the Indian background of the name. A simple one is that the Sioux Indians, who lived in the area, used the tribal name Ayuxwa, sometimes translated as meaning "one who puts to sleep." It is said that the early French spelled this "Ayoua." Fortunately the spelling gradually changed over a period of time until the word Iowa emerged, which is clearly better than everyday use than Ouaouiatonon or Ayuxwa.

Joliet and Marquette went beyond the Missouri and reached an Indian village and a tribe called Arkansea. Here they turned back, for the Spaniards had been at the mouth of the river and the little party of Frenchmen were afraid of meeting them. But they had added another name to those that would last. The French wrote it as Arkansas but, as usual, they did not pronounce the last *s* they had added.

The Frenchmen went as rapidly as possible, paddling up river to report to the governor in Montreal. Almost in sight of the town their canoe overturned, the five Indians who were with them were drowned, and all of Joliet's papers, records and maps were lost. What we know of the trip comes from Marquette's records.

But Marquette was not destined to see the results of this famous exploration. After his return, although ill, he started south again to try to found a mission. He died among the Indians living along the Lake of the Illinois that we call Lake Michigan.

Less than ten years later Robert, Sieur de La Salle, also reached the Mississippi River in his expeditions, but he went farther down. He passed the Missouri, went up the Ohio, and saw the place where the Arkansas Indians lived. La Salle had great ideas; he wanted to claim the whole area through which he had been passing for the King of France — the "Sun King" — Louis XIV. When he came to the mouth of the river on the Gulf of Mexico in 1682 he named the place in honor of the King — La Louisianne. On a post he erected the royal arms, and "in the name of the most high, mighty, invincible, and victorious Prince, Louis the Great, by the Grace of God, King of France and Navarre, Fourteenth of the name," he claimed the land for the King.

This whole vast territory, most of it never before seen by a European, was what La Salle really meant by La Louisianne. He felt that he was dedicating to the King, and claiming in his name, the whole Mississippi basin. From the Alleghenies to the Rockies, from the Gulf of Mexico to the sources of the rivers — north, east and west — was what La Salle included in La Louisianne. Although the name later applied to only that part around the mouth of the river, we still call it Louisiana.

A few years went by and the French settlers began to come into the land at the mouth of the Mississippi. They settled on both banks of the river. Those who went farthest to the east settled on a river running into Mobile Bay from the north. Here they found some Indians who may have called themselves Alpaamo, or other forms of the word. No one knows for sure what it means. The French called them Alibamons and called the river by that name as well. This later became the name of the area — Alabama.

Here, by about 1700, nine names had been recorded by the French. All but the one given by La Salle were taken from the Indians. Joliet and Marquette, La Salle and the French settlers had given a permanent stamp to the land which lies in the center of our country.

The Spanish were to try to settle there. The French did settle in many places. But before these areas could become states they had to become American. That story comes next.

For eighty years after La Salle claimed the area along the Mississippi for the French under the name Louisianne, France continued to claim the land to the east and the west of the Mississippi. Most of it they were never able to settle;

most of it, indeed, they had never seen. Then, at the close
of a long period of wars — the French and Indian Wars and
the English conquest of Canada — the French were defeated. By the Treaty of Paris in 1763 they gave to Spain
the land to the west of the great river and to Great Britain
the land to the east.

Twenty years later the Revolutionary War was won and
peace was signed. All the land held by Great Britain to the
east of the Mississippi now belonged to the United States.
The old French lands beyond the river stayed in Spanish
hands until 1800 when most of them were returned to the
French.

Then, in 1803, something very dramatic happened.
President Thomas Jefferson, who understood every maneu-
ver in the game the European powers were playing in
America, believed in the future of the United States. He
sent James Monroe to Paris to try to arrange the purchase
of all the lands along the river which were in the hands of
the French.

Napoleon was then Emperor of France. The French
colonies in the Western Hemisphere had largely been lost.
Under such conditions Louisiana by itself was of little use
to Napoleon. Moreover, he was badly in need of money. It
is said that Napoleon himself brought up the matter of a
sale. The chief statesman in France, the shrewd Talleyrand,
in a discussion of some other matters of interest with the
American minister, suddenly said, "What would you give for
all of Louisiana?" The minister was naturally startled and
excited. Since Monroe was arriving in a couple of days,
fully aware of the President's favorable attitude toward the

expansion of the country, the negotiation was deferred until his arrival.

Within a short time the matter was settled. The price for about a million acres of land, an area as large as Western Europe, was about three cents an acre. By this transaction the United States acquired all of the present states of Louisiana, Missouri, Arkansas, Iowa, Minnesota, North and South Dakota, Nebraska, Oklahoma, and most of Kansas, Colorado, Wyoming, and Montana. We call this the Louisiana Purchase.

The states of Alabama and Mississippi were under dispute for some time after the Purchase but were finally also included in the lands obtained from France.

Not all of the states gained by the Louisiana Purchase had been discovered and their names attached to the land by the French explorations we have described here. Some of these areas lay beyond their reach to the west. Nor did Michigan, Wisconsin and Illinois belong to the French although they had been explored by them and their names adapted from the Indian to the French language. These states were obtained by the United States from the British at the end of the Revolutionary War.

This territory along the Great Lakes and on both sides of the Mississippi all had Indian names except the overriding one of Louisiana. Now they were a part of the United States. Settlements by Americans began to spring up. Marquette and Joliet had begun in the north and worked down river but the lower stretches of the river grew up first.

Let's see how each of the areas grew into states.

LOUISIANA

Mississippi was made a territory before the Louisiana Purchase had brought the land west of the river into the possession of the United States in 1803. But Louisiana, which was made a territory in the year following the Purchase, achieved statehood first.

When the old "Sun King," Louis XIV, died in 1715, he had been on the throne for seventy-seven years. It was during his reign that the explorations of Joliet and Marquette and the later ones of La Salle had opened up the full length of the Mississippi. Pierre Le Moyne d'Iberville planted a colony near the present city of Biloxi on the Gulf of Mexico in the year 1699. The great age of French explorations and settlement of the land, named Louisianne in honor of this King, took place during his long reign. His influence persisted even after his death.

When he died his heir was his great-grandson, but he was so young that the Duc d'Orleans became regent; that is, he directed the kingdom until the boy was old enough to take over. Under the Duke a great company was organized to found a colony on the Mississippi; its chief city was to be called Nouvelle Orleans after the town from which he took his title.

Ready with a name for their city, the settlers voyaged to the New World, and in 1718 they founded the new city which the English later called New Orleans. Jean Baptiste Le Moyne de Bienville, brother of Pierre d'Iberville, was governor of the colony and of Louisiana. New Orleans, of course, was the seat of government. For nearly a hundred years, the area of the lower Mississippi continued to be inhabited by Spaniards, French Acadiens exiled from French Canada, and by Americans who were beginning to push toward the West.

In 1804, the year after the Louisiana Purchase, Congress cut off the more thickly inhabited lower region and called it the Territory of Orleans, from its chief town. The upper region, with its seat of government at St. Louis, was left as a vast, still-to-be-divided remainder called Louisiana. But this left the citizens of New Orleans and the surrounding area thoroughly dissatisfied. They wanted the old name back and Congress had to give in. It was 1812 when the state was admitted to the Union as Louisiana and the part to the north which had also been called Louisiana was changed by an act of Congress to be called the Territory of Missouri.

For some years after statehood was granted the seat of government remained in New Orleans. But there was a period of about six years when the nominal capital was a small town called Donaldson. Then from 1849 to 1864 Baton Rouge was the capital. Of Baton Rouge it is said that the name dates back to Pierre d'Iberville, who first colonized some areas. The story goes that the Indians had marked the boundary between two tribes by sticking a red post into the ground. The French, of course, described this as *baton rouge* — a red stick, in their language. Nearly twenty years later a military post was established there and given the name of Baton Rouge.

At the time of the Civil War New Orleans again became the capital and has always retained certain state buildings. But since 1882, Baton Rouge has been the permanent capital of the state, its Indian name a fitting one for a land once owned and inhabited not only by the original Indians but by the French, Spanish and Americans.

With this colorful history it is strange that Louisiana's only nickname is "The Pelican State." Granted that there are many pelicans along the shores and the bayous, it does seem that Louisiana has more claim to fame than this informal name suggests.

MISSOURI

After the Louisiana Purchase had settled the question of American ownership of all the French lands west of the Mississippi, great portions of this area still remained sparsely settled. One of the main trading points was a settlement made in 1763 where the Missouri and Mississippi rivers meet. This was made by the French and was called after the patron saint of the King — Saint Louis. The town, nearly half of it settled by Americans, grew in importance, using, as it did, both rivers as their access to the fur trade. The first permanent settlement, however, was at St. Genevieve, downriver from St. Louis.

When the more thickly populated Territory of Orleans was cut off from its northern portion and given the name of the chief city, the portion to the north was called simply the Territory of Louisiana. The seat of government of this area was St. Louis. We have seen how the *southern* territory was determined to return to its old name of Louisiana. This was finally granted in March, 1812. However, it was not until June 4th that Congress acted to change the *northern* part from the Territory of Louisiana, to the Territory of Missouri, named, of course, for the river which flowed through it. Because of this delay the nation had for a short time two territories called Louisiana.

Once this confusion was settled, statehood was on the way. The territory was rapidly expanding into new areas along both rivers. In 1819 the southern part of the Territory of Missouri was cut off to make Arkansas. Missouri became a state in 1821. It came into the Union as a slave state, but when the Civil War was imminent the vote in a convention called to decide their position was 80 to 1 against immediate secession. Later in 1861 the state went along with Lincoln and the Union although there were men of the state who fought for the North and others who fought for the South.

Although St. Louis had been the most important city when Missouri was a territory it had begun to select a new site for a capital a year before it had attained statehood. It was stipulated that a location near the center of the state was best, preferably near the place where the Missouri and Osage rivers joined. The site was finally determined by the close of the year and the name was chosen. President Jefferson was to be honored because he had been largely instrumental in promoting the explorations that had opened up the western parts of the state and the new lands beyond it, to the great benefit of Missouri. Explorers, traders and settlers started out from St. Louis and followed the trail through the state that had been made familiar by Lewis and Clark on their trek through unknown territory to the far West. These intrepid explorers had been sent out by President Jefferson in 1804 so it was entirely appropriate for his name to be used for the new capital — Jefferson City.

The phrase "I'm from Missouri," implying that the person speaking means "You've got to show me," has so passed into the language that many forget it is applied as a nickname to the state. Its people like to believe they can think for themselves.

MISSISSIPPI

The French, as we have seen, had given Indian names to the land, names which they took from the river, place, or tribe. The first of the new lands to be made a territory of the United States was, oddly enough, one which did not already have a name of its own. It was just called Louisiana. Still, it was east of the big river and had been ceded to the United States by the British. However, there were complications: the southern sections of both Mississippi and Alabama were still claimed by Spain as a part of what was called West Florida. In spite of this, most of the area belonged to the United States and had American as well as French settlers. In 1798 Congress called the whole area above this southern strip — West Florida — the Territory of Mississippi.

The establishment of a territory was the first step toward statehood. Usually, but not always, the name of the territory was carried over to the state. When Mississippi Territory came to be admitted as a state in 1817 there was great controversy over the use of the name. Clearly, the area was along only one small section of the river and even then only on one bank; the new state did not contain either the beginning or the mouth of the river. Yet the tradition of using the old river names was strong.

Some Congressmen thought it unreasonable to take the

name of the whole river for the small part. They proposed the name of Washington. This, however, seemed unjustified to others, who thought that no single state should pre-empt the name of the first President. (This objection was over-ruled when our farthest northwestern state was called for the "Father of His Country.") Furthermore, said some opponents of the river name, the river was not even called the Mississippi that far south. As we have seen, several tribes used different names for different parts, but the French explorers had continued the name from the north to the south no matter how many times the local tribes changed it.

Finally, by a vote of twenty-three to seventeen, Congress clung to the name Mississippi. The river name won out, as so often happened. Its nickname is "The Magnolia State," which aptly describes one of its great beauties.

Natchez was named the first territorial capital but at the time the Constitutional Convention assembled the capital had been moved to the town of Washington (proving that it was all right to name a town for the first President but not a state!). For a while this was acceptable and then the small town of Columbus was used. But this shifting of the capital became impractical. Four years after statehood was granted a committee was appointed to find a permanent site. The Pearl River runs north and south through the center of the state, and the committee explored its banks. They finally decided on a small settlement named Le Fleur Bluff, in the center of the state. When the new state house was completed and the population of the town increased, it became evident that the name was awkward and undesirable.

The final suggestion was to name it after the military hero who had beaten the British at New Orleans in the War of 1812, General Andrew Jackson. At the time the honor was given to General Jackson no one knew that they were naming their capital for the man who would be President of the United States a few years later.

ALABAMA

In the year 1540 Hernando de Soto had wandered all through the lands along the Gulf of Mexico, criss-crossing the forests northward as far as North Carolina, climbing over the Blue Ridge Mountains and the high peaks of the Appalachian system. Then he had turned south again and reached what is now southern Alabama. De Soto was a Spaniard who had made a fortune in South America and was using all of his money to explore what he expected would turn out to be very rich country, where the natives wore cloth-of-gold and lived in luxurious ease. Instead, he and his men suffered almost incredible hardships as well as disappointments.

It is true that de Soto found Indians richly dressed in feathers and furs but these were not the things de Soto could take back to Europe as prizes. Like all Spaniards he wanted gold! He also had to fight the Indians and sometimes they tricked him, as when he met Tuscaloosa, the Indian warrior chief called the Black Warrier. De Soto marched up almost alone to where the chief was seated at the top of a hill on a wooden throne. Happy in the greeting he was given, the Spaniard spent the night with the Indians, not knowing that Tuscaloosa had ordered an attack on the

Spanish soldiers. The sound of the Spanish cannon finally drove the Indians off, but this and other experiences had made de Soto's soldiers thoroughly tired of their explorations.

When de Soto got to Alabama and learned that a fleet was waiting for him on the coast, he was so determined to push on that he concealed this fact from his men and marched again into the interior. And here he died. His men built boats and escaped down the river, reaching the coast of Mexico. They left nothing behind for which they would be remembered.

The French attempted to colonize Alabama but they, too, never succeeded in making the land their own. Finally the Seven Years' War in Europe and the French and Indian Wars in America ended. When a treaty was signed in Paris in 1763 France ceded all her holdings east of the Mississippi to Britain. Twenty years later the English lost all of this to the new United States. The northern part of Alabama, some of what had originally been attached to Georgia, became American. The Louisiana Purchase finally brought the rest of Alabama to the United States, although there were endless controversies with Spain and France about this area being included in the sale.

Migration to the land lying between Georgia and Mississippi was slow but by 1814 settlers were moving in rapidly. In 1817, the year when Mississippi was changed from a territory to a state, Alabama, with its Indian name for the old tribe and the river, was cut from the huge Mississippi Territory adding the other parts from Georgia and West Florida. Congress made a new and separate territory. It was well qualified to be a territory in its own right. In 1819, after a wait of only two years, it was admitted to the Union.

Since Alabama had not previously been a separate territory it had no ready-made capital. It was not until 1847 that the city of Montgomery was chosen. That city had adopted its name to honor Major General Richard Montgomery who, in the fall of 1775, captured Montreal from the British, going north by way of Lake Champlain. Montgomery was killed in a later assault on Quebec which was led by General Benedict Arnold, then leading the American forces. Montgomery was buried in Canadian soil for nearly fifty years until America brought his body back to New York City. There he was buried and a memorial erected to him in St. Paul's churchyard. The town in Alabama, later the capital, chose the name of this true American hero.

Alabama is one of the large growers of cotton and is thus not inappropriately nicknamed "The Cotton State." But its people do not forget that their history dates back to 1540 when de Soto discovered it and its Indian king.

ARKANSAS

The Spaniard de Soto and his men, on their journey through the South in the 1500's, were the first Europeans to see what is now the state of Arkansas. But they did not give it its name. That remained to be done by the French priest Marquette and his companion Joliet. It is unlikely, however, that these Frenchmen foresaw all the difficulties the name would cause the Americans when they acquired possession of it nearly 150 years later.

The French first spelled the name as Arkansa, then to

make it plural they added an *s*. They would have pronounced it Arkánsa. The inhabitants of later years took over an approximation of the French pronunciation but they often spelled it Arkansaw, which they probably thought was nearer to the way it was pronounced. In 1819 the territory was organized and Congress formally established the name as "Arkansaw."

However, a newcomer to the territory was a printer and publisher and he, disliking what Congress had done to the word, changed the spelling back to Arkansas. Even Congress seemed to forget that it had first printed "Arkansaw" and began to use Arkansas in official documents. As time went on, people continued to spell Arkansas and to say "Arkansaw." In some printed forms it was also spelled and then pronounced — Arkánsas.

The fight went on for years. The Legislature finally took action and, more than fifty years after the state entered the Union, it appointed a committee. Whether or not the committee was biased, they settled the matter. The state was to be spelled Arkansas and pronounced "Arkansaw."

Arkansas, of course, lying as it does between Louisiana and Missouri was originally a part of the Territory of Louisiana. Later it became a part of the Territory of Missouri. However, it was separated and made the Territory of Arkansas in 1819 although it did not enter the Union until 1836.

The first settlement in the state dates back to 1686 when men who had been with La Salle settled there. In time this came to be called Arkansas Post and eventually grew into a trading center and a Jesuit mission. Large numbers of

Americans came into the area after it was purchased by the United States. When it became a Territory the first capital was the former residence of the French and Spanish governors, the early settlement of Arkansas Post.

Some years before the state entered the Union there was discussion about the selection of another capital city, some place nearer the center of the state and situated on the main river, which was also called the Arkansas. This was on the line of the traffic of traders, hunters and settlers heading toward the West.

It appears that, long before, a French expedition had traveled up the river, marking their way as they went. One of their markers was a moss-covered rock about a hundred and fifty miles northwest of the town of Arkansas Post. Another was a much bigger rock farther up the river. People began to designate them as Big Rock and Little Rock, so that a hundred years after they had first been used as guides they were well known to the community by these names.

When it became time to think seriously of a state capital it was decided to choose the little frontier village built at the site of the Little Rock, so that by the time they needed a capital they had one already named. Little Rock is still the capital.

One of the familiar names by which Arkansas is called is "Land of Opportunity." Another is "The Wonder State." It might well have as a name the "State of Something for Everybody" because each section is different from every other part. From the cypress swamps in the south to the

Ozark Mountains in the north or the rice fields in the east, the pattern changes dramatically.

ILLINOIS

The name Illinois, going back to the explorations of Joliet and Marquette, is an old one. It was to the Indian village of Kaskaskia (there is still a river of that name, which is one of the important streams in the state) that Marquette returned to found a mission after he had reported to the Governor of Canada following his first long trip down the Mississippi. Indeed, less than fifty years after the discoveries by Joliet and Marquette, the French were founding missions, making settlements, and establishing trading posts in the area of Illinois. The French claimed everything as far north as the Illinois River as part of the Province of Louisiana. This made the area readily accessible to the French in Canada.

When the lands east of the big river were deeded to the British by the French in 1763, immigration of Americans began. In fact, a few years later there were enough of them to demand a form of self-government similar to that of the colony of Connecticut. Not many years later the Governor of Virginia, a colony which claimed jurisdiction over the entire Northwest, organized all of the area as the "County of Illinois."

Some time later the British were encouraging the Indians to attack the American settlements and the frontiers of the American colonies. George Rogers Clark, brother of William Clark whom we shall hear of in another chapter, was ordered by Patrick Henry, the Governor of Virginia, to do something about it. With a handful of men he started off on his journey through flooded lands and swollen rivers. He succeeded in capturing the British posts of Kaskaskia and Cahokia in Illinois. He ended up by taking the fort at Vincennes, Indiana, where the Governor capitulated. From 1778 the Americans had much less trouble in building up their settlements in "The County of Illinois."

Illinois became a territory in 1809 but its boundaries were not those of the area we know today. It included western Indiana, most of Wisconsin, and Minnesota east of the Mississippi. The line went practically to the Canadian border.

The law required that a territory should have a population of at least sixty thousand people to qualify for statehood. In Illinois this requirement was easily met. However, nine years later when statehood was to be granted, the borders of the Territory of Illinois were redrawn. Wisconsin and the parts of Minnesota and Indiana were lopped off to leave it the state it is today. Illinois was the first of the Northern states along the Mississippi to be admitted, in 1818. There was never any question about its name.

Whether La Salle was the first Frenchman to hear the name of the marshy place at the southern tip of Lake Michigan is not well known but it is authenticated that the Algonquins called it "onion-place" because wild onions and garlic grew there in such abundance that they scented the air. The French evidently took the sound of the Algonquin word and made Chicagou out of it. The name remained for the river but a later settlement came to be called Fort Dearborn, from the less than glamorous figure of President Jefferson's Secretary of War. However, some years after Illinois was admitted to the Union the town revived the old name of Chicago for their city.

There was a small town in the center of the state called Springfield. The name may have arisen simply because there was a good spring in a field. In any case, the village grew and became the county seat of Sangamon County. There is a fascinating story of how this village became the capital of the state. It appears that there were eight prominent men in politics and one in law in Sangamon County. These men were so tall that it was said that together they totaled fifty-four feet in height. This group led the campaign for naming Springfield as the capital city. In 1837 they succeeded. Apparently one reason for their success was the convincing arguments of the lawyer of the group, a young man named Abraham Lincoln.

Illinois is nicknamed "The Prairie State" and with good reason. But it is only one of many states in the valley that would qualify for this.

MICHIGAN

For a hundred and fifty years the territory now within the boundary of Michigan was a part of New France. *Couriers du bois* or, in English, "forest runners," roamed through parts of it, missionaries tried to convert the Indians and established missions, traders came and went and the fur trade slowly developed. But there were few settlers and most of the land remained a wilderness. In fact, as late as 1815, it was officially described by the United States government as a vast swamp with only here and there a little land that was fit for cultivation.

After the Revolution the territory, along with the rest of the British possessions east of the Mississippi and south of the Great Lakes, became a part of the United States. Its boundary was fixed in rather peculiar form in 1805 when the Michigan Territory was established. The southern boundary was a neat line from the southernmost point of Lake Michigan east until it met Lake Erie. Its west boundary began at the same lower point of Lake Michigan and continued north right through the middle of the lake until it struck the northern boundary of the United States in the middle of Lake Superior. Until Alaska and Hawaii became states Michigan was the only one in the Union which was divided into two quite separate parts: the southern part has to reach the northern peninsula by water.

It was once thought that this northern peninsula was a poor exchange for cutting off a portion of the southeast corner in favor of Ohio, but the bargain proved not so bad when some of the finest iron and other minerals were later found there.

However, there was trouble ahead for the territory. In the War of 1812 the British came across the lakes and attacked Detroit. The governor of the territory, although he seems to have had more than enough men to defend the place, surrendered almost at once. Then the British proceeded to capture Mackinac and the whole territory fell into their hands.

It did not stay there long. A young naval officer named Oliver Hazard Perry was sent to Lake Erie. There he was in command of a squadron consisting of one brig, six fine schooners, and one sloop. With these vessels and a strong detachment of men sent in from the Atlantic coast, Perry soundly defeated the British squadron off a little town on the Canadian shore south of Detroit.

Contrary to the action of the governor who had given up without a struggle, Commodore Perry made a clean sweep of the British. His report in a letter to General Harrison, dated September 10, 1813, is a model of brevity that has become a famous historical quotation. He wrote, "We have met the enemy, and they are ours."

Thus Michigan returned to the United States but it was not until 1837 that it became a state. When that happened there was little doubt what the name would be, even though President Jefferson had suggested the form "Michigania" when the territory was named. However, this was forgotten by the time Congress voted for admission of the state.

Michigan has a well-known nickname. It is called "The Wolverine State." A wolverine is described in the dictionary as a blackish animal with a pale forehead and a light band on either side. It is noted for its thievishness, strength and cunning. The animal was probably chosen because it used to be prevalent in the area, not because of any similarity to the inhabitants of Michigan.

There was one oddity in the constitution of the new state. This provided that the location of the capital should be decided by legislature within twelve years. In the meantime, Detroit remained the capital.

It appeared that twelve years would be none too long for people to get together on the new location. Finally, perhaps in desperation, someone suggested a little place which had only one or two houses and a sawmill. It was named Lansing. It did not follow the pattern of other states which chose a new capital in approximately the center of the state, since Lansing was in the southern part, but at least a decision had been made and Lansing became the capital before the required twelve years had elapsed.

IOWA

Iowa is the first and perhaps the only state in the Union whose development was based on the discovery of lead mines. In 1785, a man named Julien Dubuque crossed to the western side of the Mississippi River. He was a French Canadian who had come to trade, but his discovery of the valuable mines changed his mind. He became friendly with the Indians and obtained a grant from them for twenty-one square miles. He worked the mines and formed a settlement around them. When he died in 1810 the Indians gave him the honors of a chief in the city which bore his name.

His arrival was more than a hundred years after the first French explorers and missionaries had been in the area. During this period the Indians were still in possession of the land although the Iowa Indians were forced farther west by the Indians who had been driven from Michigan by the French settlements. But the end of the Black Hawk War brought nearly 9,000 square miles of additional territory into the control of the United States which included most of what we know as Iowa. At this time the frontiersmen rushed in to mine and farm. The days of Indian control were gone. Still, the nickname of the state is "Hawkeye," apparently from a native Indian.

After the western lands were purchased from the French

by President Jefferson, the area was successively a part of Indiana Territory, of Missouri Territory, as a part of the unorganized possession of the United States, then a part of Michigan Territory and finally, for two years, a part of Wisconsin Territory. At last, in 1838, fifty years after Dubuque had found the mines, the area was separated from Wisconsin and became the Territory of Iowa, the word which had grown out of using the old name the Indians had used for an upriver tribe which they had described to Joliet. When in 1846 it became a state, the march toward the settlement of the central lands had really begun.

When the territory was named, the authorities set up a new town for a capital and called it Iowa City although it was far from being a city then. As the movement of settlers to the West became a steady flow the need for a more centrally located spot became desirable.

The record of the origin of the name Des Moines, which was that of the city they chose, is not entirely clear. It seems that Marquette and Joliet had first heard of a tribe living farther inland on a river whose name seemed to be Moingouena. The French called the river by the same name, adding, as usual, an *s*. Later, to simplify it they called it "Riviere des Moings." Still later it was written as simply Des Moines. This word might have come from the Indian name or it may mean "The Monks" as the word *moines* is French for monks or friars.

Whether Indian, French or a French adaptation, it became and still remains the capital of Iowa.

WISCONSIN

In 1634 Jean Nicolet, a French explorer, first saw the

shores of what is now Wisconsin. In 1759 the English General Wolfe captured Quebec on the famous Plains of Abraham and, the following year, the British captured Montreal. Thus for 125 years Canada and many areas south of its present border were under French control. Wisconsin remained under English rule for only twenty-three years. When the Revolution ended and the treaty was made between Britain and the United States, the lands to the south of the newly determined Canadian border were given by the defeated English to the Americans.

During all this period comparatively little settlement was made in the areas south of the three western Great Lakes of which Wisconsin was a part. Practically the whole area north of Kentucky was set aside as Indiana Territory. This included Michigan, Wisconsin, and Indiana. Then in 1816 Indiana became a state and Wisconsin was attached to Illinois. In 1818, when Illinois became a state, Wisconsin was incorporated into Michigan Territory. Then, as Michigan was about to enter the Union, Wisconsin was finally made a separate territory in 1836. In the beginning this included the present Iowa and Minnesota with a portion of North and South Dakota. From then on settlers flowed into the territory at a great rate, particularly into the southeastern portion of the state along the lake shore. But Wisconsin Territory was still spread all over the map.

At this time it was decided to set up a capital for the Territory. The rivalry of Fond du Lac, Milwaukee, Racine, Green Bay, Portage and other places was intense. At last a serious effort was made to decide on a location. Many persons spoke in favor of their village. It remained for a man named Duane Doty, a former federal district judge, to make the winning suggestion, partly, no doubt, because he had so well prepared his arguments. He produced a map and outlined all his plans for a new city in the Four Lakes region. He praised the rare beauty of its landscape. He announced that it would be called Madison, no doubt named for the fourth President of the United States, James Madison, who had died in June of that year.

Rapidly as the population grew from then on, the territory had to wait until 1848 for admission to the Union. It was still a frontier state, democratic in its attitudes, which were reinforced by an incoming German population who had left Germany in search of political freedom and democratic principles.

Wisconsin was the last of the states to enter the Union that had been under French control, intensive exploration and settlement. Its name, spelled by the first French forest-runners as "Ouisconsing" and turned into English as Wisconsin, had been its own since the earliest records of the Europeans. Like other states it had its familiar name or nickname. It is called "The Badger State." In Australia they have a similar animal but it is called a wombat or a bandicoot. Wisconsin can be thankful that the animal was called a badger in its area.

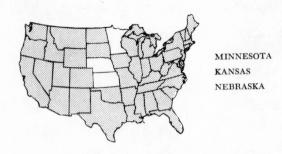

MINNESOTA
KANSAS
NEBRASKA

9. Moving Westward

The three states considered in this chapter were largely acquired by the United States as a part of the Louisiana Purchase in 1803: all of what is now Nebraska, the western part of Minnesota, and the eastern part of Kansas. At that time the area was little known even to explorers. President Jefferson sent Meriwether Lewis and William Clark to find a route to the Pacific coast. They traveled through Nebraska and Kansas. Zebulon Pike explored in Minnesota. Major Stephen H. Long surveyed parts of Kansas and somewhat later John C. Frémont, an indefatigable explorer, covered much of the same three states. None of these were very enthusiastic about the states' possibilities.

In fact, Daniel Webster spoke to Congress about the area in a way that hardly recommended it:

"What do we want with this vast and worthless area, of this region of savages and wild beasts, of deserts, of shifting sands and whirlwinds, of dust, of cactus and prairie dogs; of what use could we ever hope to put these great deserts, or those endless mountain ranges impenetrable and covered to their very base with eternal snow?"

Webster and the explorers could hardly have foreseen the endless green stretches of these three states, the vast wheat fields, the splendid livestock, the prodigious amount of food that these states produce for us, to say nothing of the iron ranges in Minnesota.

MINNESOTA

Any number of European visitors had reached the area during the two hundred years before it became a state with well-defined borders. The French had actively carried on explorations there from Canada, although sometimes their efforts would lapse for many years. During one period England controlled the northeast area above the Mississippi River but they released this land to the United States by treaty following the American Revolution. The western part was added in 1803. Twenty-eight million acres were later acquired by treaty with the Sioux Indians.

In the early days Minnesota was a part of Wisconsin Territory. Indeed, before it became a separate state it had been a part of the territories of Michigan, Missouri, Louisiana, Indiana, and Iowa as well. As a part of all these different territories it had, of course, no name of its own. When it became evident that the western part of Wisconsin, beyond the Mississippi, would be created a territory and then a state in its own right, there was great agitation about a name.

Minnesota is a land of lakes, well deserving one of its several nicknames: "The Land of 10,000 Lakes." The headwaters of the Mississippi are well up in its northern half. Logically it would be named for the Mississippi because of this. But there was already a state so named.

There was another large river in the state which the settlers called the St. Peter River but they would hardly name the state after the keeper of the Heavenly Gates. Someone then discovered that the old Sioux Indian name of the river was Menesotor or Menisothe or Menesota, meaning "cloudy water," or some say "sky-tinted water." So the inhabitants decided on Minnesota, a dignified, euphonious name.

Congress took a vote and one Congressman wanted to name it Itasca. Another suggested Chippewa. The battle went on; in fact it delayed the institution of the territory.

Finally, in 1849, the name was adopted and Minnesota was on its way to statehood, which it achieved in 1858. During the waiting period, however, the name of the St. Peter River was formally and legally changed to the Minnesota River.

The St. Peter River, however, had a counterpart when, in 1841, a Father Galtier established a mission and built a small log church at the confluence of the Mississippi and the St. Peter. When he dedicated it he said he was a resident of St. Peter's — meaning the seat of the Catholic Church in Rome — but since St. Paul is connected with St. Peter he would name the church St. Paul.

The settlement which grew up around it was called first St. Paul's Landing and later just St. Pauls. Although rivaled by the rapidly growing settlement named *Minne* (the Sioux word for water) and *polis* (the Greek word for city), which came to be spelled Minneapolis, St. Paul became and remained the capital city.

Settlement of the area was slow. A few Swiss immigrants

came in the 1820's and gradually a small village grew up in the place that was to become Minneapolis. Once the territorial status was set up and the treaty with the Sioux consummated, the news spread all over the country and immigrants poured in. Every river boat brought them, they pounded over the trails in "prairie schooners," the covered wagons later to be used on the Oregon Trail. They bought up wonderful farmland for $1.25 an acre. From a small, scattered population in 1851, when the Sioux treaty was signed, this had grown to nearly 200,000 seventeen years later.

But the problems with the Sioux were not finished. They came to believe that they had been cheated by the whites. Four years after statehood was achieved, a match was set to the kindling when the Indians killed four white men and two women. Promptly the Indians rose up. The first killings had been unplanned but they started a massacre. More than 400 men, women and children died. Finally the Indians were killed or driven off and scattered, but the shadow of the massacre hung over the settlers for generations.

On a happier note is Minnesota's claim to Paul Bunyan. This mythical "logger" is said to have roamed through the Northwest performing prodigious feats of lumbering. He was the hero of the American timberlands. As the tale of his feats grew he acquired Babe, the blue ox, who "measured forty-two ax handles and a plug of chewing tobacco between the horns." Although the legend may have originated in Canada, it was the timberlands of the Northwest which improved on his reputation year by year. Under the circumstances it is difficult for any single state to claim the birthplace of Paul Bunyan but Minnesota is probably the only state that has erected a statue to him. On the shores of Lake Bimidji in Minnesota stands a concrete statue of Bunyan eighteen feet high with Babe by his side. This is the scale on which Minnesota grows food, lumbers its forests, and mines its ore.

KANSAS

When Joliet and Marquette were exploring the Mississippi in the latter part of the seventeenth century, they heard of some Indians who lived well back from the river, toward the west. These Indians were known as *Kansa* and, as usual, the French added the *s* for the plural. The area where these Indians lived had to wait a long time before Kansas was its territorial name.

However, the Kansa Indians remained only a name, because few people had ever heard of them and still fewer had ever seen them. Coronado came up from Mexico in the middle 1500's but he did not stay long. The French drifted in and out but nothing happened. Indeed, by the time the area became a part of the United States as a result of President Jefferson's dramatic purchase of all the French claims to Louisiana, this land was still inhabited only by Indians. The general picture was one of desert, sagebrush and dry winds. In fact, the name of the Indians — Kansa — means "smoky wind" describing, perhaps, land that nobody would really want, as Brigham Young had said about the area around Salt Lake.

But the Indians wanted this arid land. The Kansa Indians seem to have been a very different type from those who lived to the north in Nebraska. They were friendly, independent and brave. Their tradition for initiating a youth into the tribe as a "brave" showed up the boy's strength or weakness. When he arrived at the age of twelve he was sent off into a lonely part of the forest. Here he had to live by his own ingenuity. When he reported back, after his lonely trial, his hardiness had been proved and he could become a full-fledged member of the tribe.

Up until the time when Kansas was finally made a territory by the Kansas-Nebraska Act in 1854 it was still an Indian land. The Kansa Indians were in possession. Many tribes from the East had been moved there as they were crowded out of more populated areas. But there were practically no settlers.

Possibly the Kansa began to feel the shadow of change hanging over them. Like many Indian tribes they loved their land. They moved about at will but they did not know the meaning of the word "own" and consequently they did not understand what the white man meant when they offered to "buy" the Indian land. A spokesman for some of the tribes tried to state this feeling about the land at the Council of Drummond Island in 1816. Their appeal still rings in our ears.

"The Master of Life has given us fish, deer, buffalo, and every kind of birds and animals for our use. . . . When the Master of Life, or Great Spirit, put us on this land, it was for the purpose of enjoying the use of the animals and fishes, but certain it was never intended that we should sell it or any part thereof which gives us wood, grass and everything."*

The following year President Monroe gave his answer:

"The hunter or savage state requires a greater extent of territory to sustain it than is compatible with the progress and just claims of civilized life . . . and must yield to it."

The Indians certainly must have seen the writing on the wall for regular caravans began schedules between Kansas and Santa Fe in the 1820's. An army of immigrants crossed the continent in their prairie schooners following the Santa Fe Trail through Kansas to California. Hunters and trappers made their way in all directions. Mormon caravans moved across the prairies to their settlement in Utah. Miners went on to better diggings. Home seekers went through, but few stayed in Kansas. Missions were established among the Eastern Indians who had been moved into the state, and the United States Army had a few frontier forts, but there were practically no permanent settlements.

Yet it was evident that all this movement affected the native Indians. They saw how their brothers had been forcibly resettled in their area and it must have been clear to the Kansa that their days were numbered. Indeed, their fears were realized. After 1854, when Kansas was made a territory, including in it much of Colorado, settlers poured in and the Indians were driven out. Kansas was granted statehood in 1861 but before that could happen it went through a most turbulent period.

* Stewart L. Udall, *The Quiet Crisis* (New York, Holt, Rinehart & Winston, 1963).

From 1854 to 1861 Kansas was the storm center of national political passions. The great question was: Should the state enter as a slave-owning state or as a free state? Missouri, on the south, was slave, her sympathies largely with the South. Kansas was divided. It became a race to see which side could move in enough immigrants to win at the polls. "Squatters" from Missouri moved up across the borders. All sorts of efforts were made to get Northerners to move in. The New England Emigrant Aid Company was particularly active and there were many others. Lawrence and Topeka were first settled by these northern immigrants or "free-staters," while Leavenworth, Lecompton and Atchison grew up as pro-slavery towns.

For some years this went on, with ballot boxes being stuffed, citizens fighting each other, armed Missourians invading Kansas, wrecking and fighting and robbing. There were reprisals by the free-state forces. A most horrible period, known as the Border War, began. John Brown (the man about whom we sing that "his body lies a-moldering in the grave but his soul goes marching on") became a fanatic abolitionist. With his sons and his neighbors, he began a campaign of retaliation on those defending slavery. He and his band murdered and mutilated five pro-slavery men. No matter how convinced people were of the rightness of Brown's purpose, they could not tolerate lawlessness and found there was little to choose between the two sides when it came to robbery, arson, pillage, the burning of homes and the driving off of settlers.

One effort after another at forming a state constitution resulted only in more difficulties. Finally one was accepted.

It made Kansas a free state. It was admitted to the Union in this form.

The territory already had a town named Topeka in an area that had good productive land. The new state chose it for its capital. The Indian meaning of the name is said to be "a good place to dig potatoes," but the land also produces sunflowers. The great golden blossoms on their tall stems stand out everywhere. No wonder it has been called the "Sunflower State."

NEBRASKA

Fifty or sixty years after the famous discoveries of the French along the Mississippi other Frenchmen went up the Missouri River. They came upon another river, broad and shallow, which they named the River Platte. In the Indian language it was the Niboapaka. Some say it sounded like *ni,* for river, and *bthaska,* meaning broad or flat. In either case it was shallow and marshy. The French name remained for the river but the Indian word moved to the land. After a while "Nibthaska" became, in English, our state name Nebraska. John Charles Frémont, who went to the area on one of his many exploring trips, is said to have been the first to give the area its more pronounceable English name.

This land had originally belonged to Spain, although Spain never really occupied the country, being interested chiefly in keeping other nations out. The Spanish lost all control after a costly massacre of a party of their troops by the Indians. In the middle of the eighteenth century two brothers named Mallet, Frenchmen from the forts on the Illinois River, crossed the state and made their way to Santa

Fe. Viewing those miles of prairie stretching to the horizon must have been an experience nearly comparable to Balboa's when he first saw the Pacific Ocean.

After its purchase by the United States in 1803, the fur trade, the search for gold in California, and the explorers brought more and more people into the area. The valley of the Platte was a natural highway to the Rocky Mountains and the western coast. This route also led many Mormons to Utah. Later, during the Civil War, Fort Kearny, located on the Platte, was the meeting place of a number of overland routes from all directions, carrying as much as 200,000 tons of freight over the trails.

Nebraska had quite a time getting its government and boundaries defined. First it was a part of Missouri Territory, then it was divided into three parts among the territories of Arkansas, Michigan and Missouri. In 1854 Congress passed an act that created the territories of Kansas and Nebraska, but the territory of the latter, as then defined, included the present state as well as parts of Montana, the Dakotas, Wyoming, and Colorado — a considerable amount of land. Not until 1863 were the present boundaries set up. It did not enter the Union until 1867.

Omaha was the capital of this territory but it was a name that was known long before it became a settlement. Joliet and Marquette, when they came to the mouth of the Missouri River on their trip down the Mississippi, had been told of some tribes of Indians who lived upstream. One of these tribes was called Maha, which stands on the earliest maps. So came the name Omaha.

As the territory grew in population, another settlement

grew up around the location of a company that was making salt, a much needed commodity in frontier towns. When the state was admitted to the Union in 1867, this town of Lancaster was chosen as the capital.

There was, however, continued discussion about the name. Eventually a Senator Patrick suggested that Lancaster be changed to Lincoln, to honor the late President of the United States who had recently been assassinated. This was unanimously adopted.

Unlike some of the prairie states farther east, there were few trees in Nebraska. Lacking lumber, men learned to build houses of sod, "soddies" they were called, which might be simple dugouts or glorified two-story structures. With the exception of a few timbers for support the entire house was made of the sod, including the roof and the floor. They were reverting, without knowing it, to dwellings not unlike those built in the Neolithic period. This shortage of wood also led them to use buffalo or cow "chips" (dried droppings of cows) for their fires. They had to contend with a shortage of water, with blizzards, hordes of grasshoppers, and dry winds. Homesteading in Nebraska certainly was not easy!

After nearly thirty years of statehood the legislature formally adopted the added term "Tree Planter's State," which shows how active they must have been during that period. How soon its nickname "The Cornhusker State" was adopted is hard to tell, but it was not a part of those sod-hut days. It came much later when the state had become a great producer of food with corn as its leading crop.

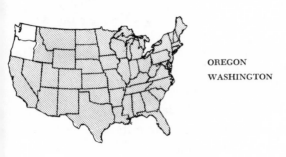

OREGON
WASHINGTON

10. The Oregon Trail

The far Northwest of our country was for a long time called just the "Oregon Country." There has been a good deal of argument about where the word "Oregon" comes from. The French Canadian word *ouragon* means storm or hurricane. The river we know as the Columbia was probably referred to as *la riviere des ouragons,* the river of squalls. Another suggestion was that Oregon comes from Aragon, a province in Spain. Still another idea is that it came from the Spanish *orejon,* meaning "big ear," an epithet which had been applied to certain Indian tribes. But this was not all. Someone suggested jokingly that the place was named after an Irishman called O'Regan!

Some historians believe that the name came from a mapmaker's mistake, that he wrote "Ouariconsint" as the name of a great river, but that part of the word was left out, leaving the word "Ouaricon," and that this later became "Ouragon" and finally Oregon.

Whatever it was called by the Indians, there were plenty of early explorers to add their bits to the name. Only twenty-five years after Cortéz entered Mexico the Spaniard,

Bartolomé Ferrelo, sailed along the Northwest coast. The area was visited by Perez, a Spanish sea captain. Other Spaniards followed. Sir Francis Drake landed on the southern coast in 1579. The Russian fur traders considered it their hunting ground. Still later came the famous Captain Cook, who visited this part of the Pacific coast before he went on to discover the Sandwich Islands — which we now know as Hawaii. The fur traders and the British from Canada were pushing down into the area.

But it was Captain Gray who gave us the name which became an important part of the territory. From Boston to what is now Portland, Oregon, is a journey we can now measure in hours. But when Captain Robert Gray made the trip in 1788 it was only after months of sailing and beating around Cape Horn that he came to the mouth of a large river, which he christened the Columbia, after his ship. His discovery established our first claim to all the land which the river drained.

We have no reliable report as to whether anyone crossed the continent from the East to the Northwest during that period. But Thomas Jefferson, after the Louisiana Purchase, decided to find a way overland. Meriwether Lewis was his secretary, but he was also an explorer, so the President appointed him to lead an expedition in search of a route to the Pacific. William Clark went with him.

We know the trip as the Lewis and Clark Expedition. Setting out from St. Louis, where they worked out their plans during an entire winter, they traveled up the Missouri River, crossed the mountains and finally struck the Columbia River. They followed this until they reached its mouth, where Captain Gray had given it its name a dozen years before.

This was part of the route which came to be called the Oregon Trail. It was a trail made not only by Lewis and Clark but by trappers as well as other explorers and the Indians. In 1842 the first immigrant train went through. From then on thousands of pioneers, seeking new lands, drove their horses and oxen over it. The journey was certainly a long, long trail — over 2,000 miles long. It started at Independence, Missouri, and followed the North Platte River and its tributary, the Sweetwater. It went through the south pass of the Rocky Mountains, and then through Fort Laramie, Independence Rock and Salt Lake to Oregon City.

These places had no names when Lewis and Clark first saw them. Many of them were recorded by these first explorers. Some of them received their names from the settlers as the wagons moved slowly along through drought and storm. Their household goods were packed in with their families, their cattle and horses walked alongside, their plows and harrows were lashed to the wagons. They met and overcame Indians. They braved the dangers of mountains and rivers. Not all who started reached the promised land.

Without their wagons they would never have made it. These wagons we know as "covered wagons" and as "prairie schooners." They were originally known as Conestoga wagons. Conestoga is an Indian word meaning "the place of the muddy waters." It had been given to a town near Lancaster, Pennsylvania, where the Conestoga wagons, with their broad iron tires, were first built.

The settlers came and made the land blossom. The traders came and the British came. In fact, from 1818 until 1846 the British and the United States ruled the land jointly. Not until then was the international boundary established at the 49th parallel which separated the Oregon Territory from Canada.

OREGON

Two years later, the land safely a part of the United States, a government for the Territory of Oregon was set up. The name was applied to the whole area from the Rocky Mountains to the ocean, north of the California-Nevada line.

Then began the first moves to break up the huge expanse of land in the territory and make its parts ready to move toward statehood. The part below the Columbia River, into which settlers had been coming since the Oregon Trail had opened up, remained Oregon Territory. Within a few years they had voted for statehood and in 1859 this became the thirty-third state to enter the Union. For them there was no question of a name — it was Oregon.

There were no large cities in Oregon when the time came to name a capital. Most of the people had settled in the area along the coast and in the lovely valley of the Willamette River. Here was a community that was the outgrowth of the work of Jason Lee, a missionary who had been sent there by the Methodist Episcopal Church. As early as 1842 he had founded a school which grew into what is now Willamette University. The village that grew up around the mission was named Salem. It was chosen as the capital the year after the new state was admitted to the Union.

But Oregon went back to the old days for its nickname. By the early 1800's Oregon Country was the end of the trail for the fur traders who had been working their way through the West and coming down from the North. Beaver was king, largely because men of any pretensions to fashion wore hats made of beaver skins. No wonder the state later adopted the nickname "Beaver State."

Oregon and California, which had come into the Union a few years before, were all alone out there on the coast 3,000 miles from the seat of the federal government. There was no state between them and Texas, which had come in a few years earlier, and Minnesota which had been admitted only the year before Oregon. News did not travel fast across such great wastes and it was equally slow by steamer around the tip of South America or transferring from one steamer to another by road across the Isthmus of Panama. It was a month before Oregon knew that the papers making it legally a state had been signed.

WASHINGTON

All land drained by the Columbia River was called the Oregon Country or the Northwest. But the Columbia is a very large and a very long river, with many tributaries. Many states were to be founded in this area.

The coastline of the area is deeply indented; indeed, one western section is almost cut off from the mainland, making a great peninsula. High mountains border the coast but the shoreline is long and the harbors are many and large. All the early sea captains, Spanish and English, explored the coast. One of the earliest, Juan Perez, saw a very high, snow-clad peak which he named Santa Rosalia. So far as is known, Perez was the first European to look upon a part of what is now Washington State.

A few years later, in 1788, came Captain John Mears, an Englishman who crossed the various waterways and re-named the mountain, Mount Olympus, after the mythical home of the Greek gods. Although he searched for the legendary river that had been reported running from east to west across the country, and he entered the bay into which the Columbia flows, he did not find the mouth of the river. With wry humor he named the inlet Deception Bay and the headland Cape Disappointment. The discovery of the river, of course, was made by Captain Gray four years later.

Lewis and Clark entered Washington from Idaho by the Snake River, which led them to the Columbia. But settlers did not rush to the northern part of Oregon Country as they had to the southern part. Since all the land was in dispute with the British, the Hudson's Bay Company discouraged Americans from coming into the area north of the Columbia. Until an agreement was made with the British there was not a single successful settlement north of the river.

The first permanent American settlement was made on Puget Sound in 1845. Two years later another town a few miles away was started and named Smithfield. A few Americans thus defied the British and began the slow build-up of population.

A few years before Oregon gained statehood the people north of the Columbia River petitioned Congress to be "organized as a separate territory under the name and style of the Territory of Columbia." This was following a practice with which they were long familiar — naming a state for a large local river.

The name was popular and was about to be accepted by Congress, when there was an objection. A Congressman from Kentucky urged that the name Washington be used instead, thus revealing a change of mind in the position of some in Congress in connection with Mississippi. He said that one of our states should honor the Father of His Country. Another Congressman stated in rebuttal that it would cause confusion: there were already so many places called Washington "that it is almost impossible when you hear the name of a town to know in what part of the world it is." (There was a good deal in what he said. Even a few years ago there were over thirty counties named Washington, nearly four hundred communities, ten lakes, seven mountains and over a thousand streets, to say nothing of our capital city.)

The nickname of "The Evergreen State" is an understated description of the beauty of the state. Mountains tower 14,000 feet above the gentle coastal plains; there are rain-drenched forests and huge glaciers. Yet the climate along the ocean is mild enough so that the area remains green with blooming flowers all the year around. Sometimes called "The Switzerland of America," which might have been a more accurate description, it is one of our most beautiful states.

The people who wanted to call their state Columbia would have been much better pleased if they had been allowed to do so. Over the protests of the citizens and of those who supported them, Columbia was dropped and the Territory of Washington was accepted. For the capital of their territory they went to the little town of Smithfield which had been started only five years earlier. They renamed it Olympia. It remained the capital when, in 1889, the territory was admitted to the Union.

The tradition of adopting a name because of its local significance and the desire of its citizens had been abandoned for the first time. We shall probably never have a state that, even indirectly, honors Columbus.

THE DAKOTAS
IDAHO
MONTANA
WYOMING

11. The States Between

The North American continent was settled by fits and starts: first by the Spanish in Florida and the Southwest in the early 1500's; then the French trekked through Canada and the Great Lakes and at last worked their way down the Mississippi to the Gulf 150 years later; in the meantime the English had come to the East Coast and from Maine to Georgia had dug in to stay.

That was the difference between the nations. The Spanish remained and colonized Mexico but their explorations north of the present United States border resulted in no lasting settlements. The French explored and colonized around the Gulf of Mexico but along the thousand miles of river they gained only a few permanent footholds.

But the English came to stay. The people who braved the months on the Atlantic crossing brought their household goods with them and came to build permanently. In the end it was the English and, after the Revolution, the Americans who explored the continent; the homeseekers followed after them.

Where there were only Indians, the Americans moved in.

161

When they came to territory claimed by the French, they staked out a home anyway, and began clearing the land and plowing. When they were ready to move into the Southwest they did so despite the political claims of the Spanish. They fought the Indians and drove them out; they fought the British not only to assert the freedom of the Thirteen Colonies but they also gained possession of the land farther west to the Mississippi. They bought out the French. They fought the Spanish to gain Texas and later won from them everything west to California.

The settlements of the English and the Americans moved in waves but not always connecting waves. By the time the United States had won its freedom from the British its people had struck their roots deeply into the soil of the area from Maine to Georgia and for a distance of two hundred miles or so inland from the coast. In the nearly two hundred years since colonization began they had made this land their own.

The treaty with the British which gave the Americans rights as far west as the Mississippi at once generated a new westward movement. Through Kentucky, Tennessee, Ohio and Arkansas they pushed their way, driving out the Indians and replacing the scattered French. They worked their way along the lands south of the Great Lakes.

Then came the next wave following the Louisiana Purchase in 1803. Now the Americans were free to cross the Mississippi and gather into their hands other areas previously claimed by the French.

Lewis and Clark followed the Missouri River from St.

Louis to a point near the present Bismarck, North Dakota, where they spent the winter. They traversed both North and South Dakota, Montana and the north spur of Idaho; they crossed the mountains and went down the Columbia River.

Forty years after this great adventure, Americans were moving to the Pacific Northwest, bypassing the lands between. The Oregon Trail through Nebraska and Wyoming provided passage for the covered wagons to Oregon Territory. The Santa Fe Trail opened the doors to California. The acquisition of lands formerly owned by Mexico made the Southwest available to Americans for the first time. Prior to that Americans had moved on into Texas when men pushed across the line from Louisiana and Arkansas in the 1830's.

Then, always moving west, the states of Minnesota, Nebraska and Kansas were organized. The Indians were routed and the pioneers moved in. Wave after wave of Americans had spread out to set up new homes.

Only one part of the continental United States remained largely unknown except to hunters, trappers and traders. These were the lands that had been left behind by the leap to the coast and had not yet been reached by the overland push from the East. The unexplored and uninhabited areas from the Dakotas westward to Oregon Territory were the last frontier. Not until the Indians had been subdued and killed or relocated did these areas become available to immigrants. Not until the railroads began to come through about 1870 did people crowd into the Dakotas, gradually spreading out farther west. The railroads not only brought newcomers but also carried out the gold they dug and the products of their agriculture.

THE DAKOTAS

The area known as Dakota was inhabited by the Dakota Indians, a subdivision of the Sioux. These Indians were relatively friendly; fur traders had been in and out for years. The Dakotas were a handsome people, later to be immortalized on an issue of American pennies and nickels. When the land was made a territory in 1861 it was natural that the name of the local Indians be used.

The southern and northern parts of the state were in many ways quite different. The southern part owed its development largely to the Missouri River which, starting in St. Louis, became the natural highway for fur traders. A Frenchman named Joseph La Framboise (the name means "raspberry") had followed the river northward and built Fort Teton only ten years or so after Meriwether Lewis had been there. The present site of Pierre is on the opposite side of the river from the old fort, the first settlement in South Dakota. Steamboats began to ascend the Missouri in 1831 and the fur trade grew.

Pierre became the capital of the state fifty-seven years later, replacing Yankton, a town on the southern boundary of the state. Pierre was named for Pierre Choteau, who, with his brother August, had founded the city of St. Louis and built up a great fortune trading with the Northwest Indians.

The first people who came to stay stopped at the falls of

the Sioux River in the southeast corner of what is now South Dakota. This was in 1856, the immigrants coming from Minnesota and Iowa. But the population grew slowly until, in 1874, gold was discovered by General Custer's men in the Black Hills of the southwest corner of the state. Men in search of gold rushed in from everywhere — but the mining prospects petered out. However, more prospecting was done further north and rich workings were discovered at Deadwood Gulch. Then came the big find, in 1876, when the Homestake lode was discovered. This has remained one of the word's greatest gold mines.

After that the "Dakota Boom" was on, every county began to fill up and agitation for statehood reached its height. The southern half of Dakota wanted to make Dakota Territory into two separate states. It also made every effort to claim the name Dakota for itself but was unable to make it stick. The Committee on Territories declared that the name Dakota was as dear to the people of the northern part as it was to those in the south. Furthermore, the northern part claimed that the wheat it grew, along with its other grain crops and cattle, had become famous all over the world. Its inhabitants were not going to part with the name Dakota.

At this point someone probably remembered that the Indian name Dakota really meant "friend." If that was the case it would hardly do to strain the meaning of their word for friendship by forcing either side to give up the name. Both sides agreed to North Dakota and South Dakota, still friends, but separate states. They were both accepted into the Union in 1889.

North Dakota differed in many respects from South Dakota. It was first settled by Scottish Highlanders from Canada in 1813. When the railroads began to come through in the 1870's, groups of immigrants came not only from Canada but also from as far away as Europe. More than forty foreign countries were represented in its population. Indeed, it is said that because North Dakota wanted to attract the Germans they named their capital city Bismarck, in honor of the Iron Chancellor of Germany. This may have attracted German immigrants but it gave North Dakota a somewhat overpowering air.

North Dakota had its great grain fields in the rich, fertile river valleys. Livestock of all species roamed its meadows. The immigrants were frugal and industrious and they made every field productive.

North Dakota is known for its ground squirrels. These burrowing animals resemble the chipmunk. The popular name for them was "flickertail," which led to the nickname "The Flickertail State." This may not mean much outside of North Dakota but to the people of the state it has a familiar ring.

South Dakota calls itself "The Sunshine State," which puts it ahead of North Dakota in appeal except that its second nickname is "Coyote State."

IDAHO

The name Idaho seemed to hold a fascination for Congress. Many delegates had wanted to use the name for the state they eventually decided to call Colorado. When it came time to name the huge territory which at that time included the states of Idaho, Wyoming, and Montana, plus parts of Nebraska and the Dakotas, Mr. Ashley, the powerful Chairman of the Committee on Territories, was all for naming it Montana. Bitter exchanges took place. Apparently many of the legislators knew little about the names they were talking about.

Idaho might come from the name used by a tribe of Indians for the Comanche. This was "Idahi." But the Shoshonean language also had a word that sounded somewhat like the other. In their language *ee-dah-how* meant something like the English "good morning." It is also reported that the word "Idahi" is the Shoshonean name for the purple columbine, a flower growing in great fields in Colorado. Still another authority says that Idaho was the name of the Salmon River tribe of Indians. *Ida* means salmon and *ho* means tribe, so that we might be saying "salmon eaters." The most popular meaning, however, was one which many authorities doubt that it ever had. Most people seemed to believe it meant "Gem of the Mountains," but this is considered by some to be unlikely. However, it is this phrase, or its shortened form, Gem State, that Idaho adopted as its nickname.

In any case, Idaho began to be used all over the area but Congress still wrangled between Idaho and Montana. Finally, in spite of certain preferences for Montana, Idaho was chosen when the new territory was organized.

Idaho was a part of "Oregon Country," disputed among Russia, Spain, Great Britain, and the United States. The United States' claim rested largely on Lewis and Clark, the first known white men in the state. A later explorer was

Andrew Henry, a fur trader, who built Henry's Fork in 1810. This was the first building ever erected by an American west of the Continental Divide. Then came Wilson Price Hunt. He and his company were sent out by John Jacob Astor to get to the mouth of the Columbia River so they could trade for furs. They were the first party to make the trip along the route followed later, in the main, by the Oregon Trail. All of these explorations involved fantastic dangers and adventures. None but the hardy could have made them.

For thirty-five years after the War of 1812, Idaho was controlled by the British. The result was continuous efforts by the English Hudson's Bay Company and American explorers to overthrow each other.

In one such effort the British built Fort Boise. The name came from a band of French fur trappers who had crossed the Oregon Country. When they reached water and shade trees they exclaimed *les bois*, meaning "the trees" in French. The name was later corrupted by the English to Boise. Fort Boise served as a hostelry for the travelers on the Oregon Trail. Later, as a town grew up around it, it became the capital of the state.

As was true in the other "in between" states, thousands of people passed over the trail to the coast but few remained in the land. The American Board of Foreign Missions had sent a man and his wife there to minister to the Indians in 1836. This was the first home of any white family in the area. The Mormons tried one mission which failed because of the hostility of the Shoshone Indians. However, a second one just over the boundary from Utah succeeded.

As was the case of other states in this area it was the discovery of gold that brought immigrants. The first discovery was made in 1860 along a tributary of the Clearwater River. More gold was discovered shortly thereafter in the Boise basin. Within two years there were 16,000 persons in the basin. Other discoveries confirmed Eastern capital in their opinion that here was a good thing and the state was off to a fine start.

It was also a beautiful state. While there are a few valleys in the southern part, most of the state is mountainous. It has magnificent falls, one of which is higher than Niagara. The Bitterroot Range follows the whole eastern border of the state. There are many other high ranges. Mt. Borah, nearly 13,000 feet, is the highest point in the state. Because of this topography the state was never fully settled and much of it is still inaccessible except on foot or horseback.

In 1863 the territory was organized but it was never again so large, for, as we know, a number of territories were carved out of it to form other states. When it entered the Union in 1890 its boundaries were fixed.

The first legislature met in Lewiston, just on the border of Washington, but southern Idaho men became more dominant and insisted on moving the second legislature to Boise, where the capital has remained ever since.

MONTANA

The persistent Mr. James M. Ashley, Chairman of the Committee on Territories, was not a man to give up easily. He had been defeated on the decision to use the name Idaho for the state that was made a territory in 1863 but his chance came the next year. It was decided to divide the Territory of Idaho and make its eastern half into a new state. Ashley again had his opportunity which he immediately took advantage of by introducing a bill to name the new territory Montana.

The word, both in Latin and Spanish, means "mountainous" and the term was applicable at least to the western part of the new state. The eastern portion was made up of plains and rivers. These two so different sections were both to contribute to the ultimate wealth of the state. The western part with its mining, the eastern with its agriculture. But it was for the mountains that it was to be named and this time Mr. Ashley had his way. In 1864 Montana became official. At that, the state barely missed being named Abyssinia, a country in North Africa. Someone suggested that it should have an Indian name, and the man who was challenged to name one came out with Abyssinia.

As in all these states, the fur traders came first. For nearly half a century the fur trade dominated the region. After 1850 some settlers trickled into the Bitterroot Valley but, like its neighbors, the area did not attract much attention until gold was discovered. In 1858 two brothers made the first gold strike. Three years later a much richer strike was made on Grasshopper Creek, and the rush was on. Then gold was discovered at Alder Gulch. Virginia City grew up around it. Here the first newspaper in the state was published. The names of these localities spread across the country and more and more prospectors arrived.

The take was fabulous. The find spread from gulch to gulch. The number of miners increased. This brought about difficulties with the Indians. General George A. Custer led the federal troops against the Indians in 1876. He lost his life in an attack when the Indians wiped out his forces, but by the following year the Indian troubles in Montana had largely ended.

Custer, a veteran of the Union Army, had a great deal of understanding of the Indians he was fighting. He said, "If I were an Indian, I often think I would prefer to cast my lot among those of my people who adhered to the free open plains, rather than to submit to the confined limits of a reservation." That the Indians felt great pride in their country and a full appreciation of why they wanted to keep it, is shown in a statement made by the Crow chief, Arapooish, which Stewart Udall gives in his book, *The Quiet Crisis.*

> "The Crow country is exactly in the right place. It has snowy mountains and sunny plains; all kinds of climate and good things for every season. When the summer heat scorches the prairies, you can draw up under the mountains, where the air is sweet and cool, the grass fresh, and the bright streams come tumbling out of the snowbanks. There you can hunt the elk, the deer, and the antelope, when their skins are fit for dressing: there you will find plenty of white bears and mountain sheep.

> "In the autumn, when your horses are fat and strong from the mountain pastures, you can go down into the plains and hunt the buffalo, or trap beaver in the streams. And when winter comes on, you can take shel-

* Stewart L. Udall, *The Quiet Crisis* (New York, Holt, Rinehart & Winston, 1963).

ter in the woody bottoms along the rivers; there you will find buffalo meat for yourselves, and cottonwood bark for your horses; or you may winter in the Wind River Valley where there is salt in abundance.

"The Crow country is exactly in the right place. Everything good is to be found there. There is no country like the Crow country."

The Americans were taking the land from the original inhabitants who loved it. After the Indian question was settled, rightly or wrongly, the eastern half of the land began to develop rapidly. The first drive of cattle from Texas to the Montana ranges was in 1869. The sheepherder was coming into his own, shipping his wool down the Missouri and the Mississippi to New Orleans.

Gold and silver mining kept pace with the discovery of new lodes and the development of the old ones. Then an entirely new source of wealth was discovered. In working a silver deposit which began to peter out, Marcus Daly discovered the "richest hill in the world" which was full of copper. Daly named his find the Anaconda, apparently taking the name by chance from a newspaper that said that Grant's army was encircling that of Lee "like a giant anaconda." The Anaconda mine is still one of the world's richest sources of copper.

All of these developments made Montana ripe for statehood in 1889. Its capital, Helena, was built up around the Last Chance Gulch mine, discovered in 1864, the same year that Montana was made a territory. In fact, the Last Chance Gulch ran right down the main street of Helena.

Officially, Montana has a nickname that portrays the state

perfectly. It is called "The Treasure State," which indeed it was. But it was also dubbed "The Stubtoe State," because of the number of former Confederate soldiers in their broad-toed boots who came to recoup their fortunes in the gold fields.

WYOMING

Like all the states referred to in this chapter, Wyoming got its start through the fur traders. A number of free trappers and employees of the various St. Louis fur companies worked the area. After 1824 several hundred traders crossed the South Pass of the Continental Divide — the high point from which waters flow both to the west and the east. They came to a meeting which became an annual event. Here a colorful frontier gathering of Indians, fur traders and company employees convened to meet the pack trains of the company and exchange the furs which they had brought for the supplies the company was furnishing them. Hundreds of tents and tepees dotted the river bottoms during this meeting, the Indians were in full regalia, the traders in buckskins.

The real magnet for the trappers was beaver. The mountain men came to be "free-trappers" in the 1820's, but few of them got rich at it and most died poor. Beaver pelts sold for six dollars each in good years. It took a good man to make a thousand dollars a year.

The first white man known to have entered the state was John Colter, who had been with Lewis and Clark. He left them on their homeward trip and went back into the wilderness to trap for himself. It was he who first became familiar with the northeastern corner of the state and the phenomenon of the section we call Yellowstone Park. His almost unbelievable tales of its wonders were the first news of this area that came to the outside world.

But men who trapped learned to know the mountains. Not for nothing were they called "Mountain Men." When the wagon trains began to roll out across the plains in the '40's and '50's the "White Indians" came to the aid of the immigrants, helping them to find water holes, to avoid ambushes and to keep moving.

Still, Wyoming was a place through which people passed rather than one where they stayed. The Oregon Trail was first in use in 1842. The Mormon migration was added a few years later and after that came the Gold Rush to California in '49. This was also the route of the famous Pony Express and the stage coaches which followed it through Wyoming.

But it was the railroad that opened up the land to permanent settlement. When the Union Pacific Railroad began to lay its tracks across the state in 1876, the rush was on. The Territory of Wyoming was organized in 1868. This brought up the problem of naming it. The argument was so bitter and prolonged it almost caused a break-up of the Houses of Congress.

There was a beautiful valley in Pennsylvania in the old days which the Delaware Indians called, in their language, "at the big flats." The Indian name was long and difficult; the white settlers called it Wyoming. But in 1778 a band of Indians defeated the settlers and massacred more than three hundred of them. In spite of the bad name this gave the place, a poet of the time wrote about it and the name became popular.

Some of the men in Congress were in favor of naming the new territory Wyoming, although none could explain why a name from the East, with such unpleasant associations, should be transplanted to the far West. Even the meaning "big flats" was hardly appropriate for a state with so many mountains. The lengthy debate was the longest ever to take place in the Congress about a name for a state.

At last, after considering all sorts of Indian names, it was finally decided to accept Wyoming. This apparently was because the delegates and Congressmen liked the way it sounded when they rolled it out in a speech. Wyoming really got its name because of its oratorical appeal.

Cheyenne had been one of the names suggested and refused for the state but it came into its own as the name of the capital. When the railroad was being built through Wyoming, Major-General Dodge selected the site of one of his field camps for a terminus. He chose a name from the Algonquin tribe of the Plains Indians and called it Cheyenne. So the state got a name from its own Indians even if the state's own name came from "back East." The official librarian at Cheyenne insists that the correct pronunciation is "Shy Ann."

When at last settlers began to come in a few years after territorial status was granted, they found that the grass of the plains furnished excellent feed for cattle. Irrigation was provided by hundreds of streams and snows made it possible for herds to live all winter without extra food or care. Texas, which was greatly overstocked, began to drive vast herds along the trail to Wyoming to roam and eat until they were ready to be driven to the railroad.

In those days the cowboys kept the beasts on the trail by singing to them. The song they used most often is still with us:

> Whoopee ti yi yo, get along little dogies,
> For you know Wyoming will be your new home.

But the cattlemen put too many cattle on the ranges so that there was not enough feed during the winter. As a result, many thousands died. By 1890, when Wyoming became a state, the cattle business was in decline but sheep raising was proving profitable.

The nickname of the state is "Equality State" for a reason that makes it unique among states and probably in the world. At the time of its first territorial legislature, in 1869, women were given the right to vote in all elections. That right was never withdrawn and gives Wyoming a "first" of major distinction.

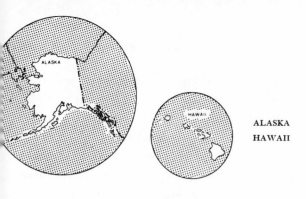

ALASKA
HAWAII

12. Arctic to Tropic

In 1912 the admission of two states — Arizona and New Mexico — brought the number of states in the Union to forty-eight. The land from Maine to California, from Washington to Florida, was one solid block of states with equal rights and equal responsibilities. All the territories had graduated from their secondary status.

For forty-seven years thereafter no new state was added. Then two territories which had waited — one for fifty-nine years (Hawaii), one for forty-seven years (Alaska), achieved the statehood they desired.

For the first time we had gone outside our solid block of contiguous states, stretching across the center of the continent, to grant equal status to a peninsula jutting from the northwestern part of the continent. The western tip of Alaska is as far west of San Francisco, California, as that city is west of Portland, Maine. In fact, the string of the Aleutian Islands stretches into the Eastern Hemisphere, the only part of the United States to do so.

We had done the same to bring statehood to a group of islands sitting out in the middle of the Pacific Ocean more than 2,000 miles from San Francisco and about one-third of the way from California to China.

These two new states are very different from each other. The fact that they are also different from the older states on the mainland is of no importance. The mainland states also differ: Wyoming, for example, is about as different from Florida or even from New Mexico as is possible. The United States has had the ability to assimilate all kinds of different states and different peoples. The addition of the new states has served to further this diversification.

ALASKA

In the early 1700's, while we were busy settling ourselves on the land along the Atlantic coast, the Russian Czar in St. Petersburg became interested in some stories about the land beyond the farthermost eastern part of his realm — the tip of Siberia. It was even said that there might be land connecting Siberia and America. Vitus Jonassen Bering, a Dane, made two trips into the area. In the first one he decided that the sea separated Asia from North America. The strait through which he sailed bears his name even today. On the second trip, after many disasters, he died. Nevertheless, voyages which followed led to much information about the land, the people, the animals, and the furs that were to be gotten there.

About the time of the American Revolution, when Catherine the Great ruled Russia, she too heard stories. These concerned large herds of mysterious sea-going animals on islands about 200 miles north of the Aleutians. These were the seal islands, later named the Pribilof Islands.

The Russians plunged into the seal-hunting business and also started colonizing not only the long string of the Aleutian Islands but the mainland as well. Their brutal treatment of the natives — both Eskimos and Indians — made them extremely unpopular.

For many years Russia claimed the land. Then, in 1867, the United States stepped in and bought Alaska from the Russians for $7,200,000. The deal was negotiated by William H. Seward, Secretary of State. For a long time this purchase was called "Seward's Folly" because what he had bought was a far-off, unknown, largely uninhabited land. Thirty years later no one could call it folly, because gold was discovered in 1896-97 on the Klondike River. From then on a flood of Americans went to Alaska to dig up the gold. They found more and more. Although not everyone made his pile — and many died trying — when the rush began to peter out, the area had a population of Americans who remained and developed the country.

In 1912 Alaska was made a territory of the United States. This area has a very peculiar shape. Cut off from the Yukon Territory of Canada by a straight north-south line, it then wanders on down the edge of British Columbia in a narrow strip bordered by deep inlets and many islands. This boundary was finally determined in 1903 by a tribunal of British and American jurists.

It is on this southern strip that the town of Juneau grew up. This was chosen as the capital of the territory. It is still the capital — a city of only some 7,000 people.

The name Alaska is derived from the Aleutian language, which is that of the Eskimos of the Alaskan peninsula. This peninsula is that part of the mainland that juts out toward the eastern end of the Aleutian chain. The name in their language is *Alaxsxaq,* and it is just as well we do not have to use it. The Russians translated it somewhat as we do so that the name Alaska has been applied to that land for a long time.

Over the years there were repeated efforts to acquire statehood for the territory. In 1959 these efforts finally matured. In January of that year Alaska became our forty-ninth state. The population was then nearly a quarter of a million in an area of nearly 600,000 square miles. This area is greater than that of the original thirteen states. It is, of course, thinly populated, most of the towns being in the southern part.

One of the greatest problems the territory and the state have had to deal with is transportation. All supplies had to come in by boat until airplane shipping and air passenger traffic began to take some of the load. More roads have been built and in the 1940's the new Alcan Highway was constructed by agreement between Canada and the United States.

Alaska has a number of other claims to fame among our fifty states. It has Mt. McKinley, a 20,300-foot-high mass that is the highest peak in America. It has a climate that is moderated by the warm Japanese Current along the coast but which inland sometimes drops as low as 70 degrees below zero. It is our only "Land of the Midnight Sun." It has one of the great rivers of the world, the Yukon, which is navigable by steamers for over 2,000 miles. One might say that Alaska has almost everything.

Alaska can be summed up by the last two lines of the poem "Alaska's Flag."

> Alaska's flag — to Alaskans dear,
> The simple flag of a last frontier.

HAWAII

The name of our fiftieth state is as old as the Polynesian race, and no man knows quite how old that is. James Ramsey Ullman, in a book about the South Pacific islands,* says, "In the beginning there was Havaiki. Anthropologists have placed it in Malaya, India, Persia, as far west as the shores of the Red Sea and the coasts of Africa. . . . The people themselves — the brown migrant people who have become known as the Polynesians — do not know. They know only that in all their legends, all their traditions, the place of their ancient origin is called Havaiki. . . . Raiatea, near Tahiti, was once known as Havaiki. So was Savaii, the largest of the Samoan Islands. And so — with the least change through the centuries — was America's Hawaii."

Hawaii, therefore, was home, whether one left it or went to it. How long ago Hawaii became home to the Polynesians who reached its shores in huge canoes can only be estimated. Most research suggests that the migrations of the race began nearly fifteen hundred years ago and that the Polynesians have been in the Hawaiian Islands for at least a thousand years.

Probably the first European discoverer of the islands was

* *Fia, Fia* by James Ramsey Ullman, The World Publishing Co., 1962

Captain James Cook, who arrived there in 1778, at which
time he named them the Sandwich Islands after his patron,
the Earl of Sandwich. He was cordially treated by the
natives. On his second trip, the next year, trouble developed
and Cook was killed. A year or two later Kamehameha had
made himself the king of the largest island, named Hawaii,
and had taken over power in most of the rest of the islands.
His dynasty ran in a straight line for ninety years.

During the early part of his reign American missionaries
began to arrive. In 1820 these good people were admitted
by the King and given every opportunity to start their
labors to convert the islanders.

Over the years they did much more than that. They and
the other Americans who followed them became not only
the bearers of religion but they brought an entire change in
the way of life. They opened schools, they taught the
people to read and write and to speak English. They
brought in the first printing press, they introduced
European forms of clothing, and they introduced the cultivation of sugar cane. They were advisers to the government and, as time went on, they introduced and carried on
the industry and commerce of the islands.

In the meantime the French and the English had made
efforts to establish themselves, but the Americans had become too firmly entrenched. As early as 1849 a treaty was
prepared that would bring Hawaii into the American union
as a state on a "perfect equality with the other states of the
Union." This was never signed because of the death of
Kamehameha III, but the objective was rarely lost sight of.

During the 1800's great changes were taking place in the population. Estimates of the native population at the time of Captain Cook's arrival were about 300,000. By 1836 this had dropped to slightly over 100,000. It continued to drop. By the end of the nineteenth century there were only 39,000 native Hawaiians left. Nearly one-quarter of the population was Japanese while almost as many were Chinese. There were large numbers of Portuguese and a number of other Europeans but there were still only a few thousand Americans. Yet the inhabitants never ceased asking to be a part of the United States.

In 1900 this finally came to pass. In June of that year an Act of Congress set up the Territory of Hawaii. Under this form of government the people were American citizens with all their rights as such, but they could not achieve statehood. In 1935 they tried, but were defeated in Washington. Again in 1937 the matter was under consideration.

Statehood opponents found fresh ammunition in the 1940 Census. The Territory then had a population of 424,000, but nearly forty per cent of it was Japanese. The war in Europe was in progress and relations with Japan were steadily deteriorating. The American legislators raised their voices to question the loyalty of these citizens, most of whom were second or third generation Americans by birth. All such doubts were more than silenced by the contribution of the battalions of "Americans of Japanese ancestry" from Hawaii. No outfits fought more bravely or sustained greater losses.

Pearl Harbor did more than prove the loyalty of its

Oriental citizens. As the Senate committee which recommended passage of an Hawaii statehood bill said, "Pearl Harbor, for all its tragedy, served one grimly useful purpose. It made the United States aware that its western front was not the coast of California, but a group of islands some 2,000 miles southwestward in the Pacific."

So the statehood drive was resumed. In 1947 and again in 1950 bills were presented. In 1953 the matter came up again. Since 1903 when the first appeals for the change from territory to statehood were made, twenty-four hearings had been held on the claim. No state ever waited longer or tried harder to gain admission than did these Pacific islands.

Finally on March 18, 1959, President Eisenhower signed the bill, passed by both Houses of Congress, that Hawaii had been granted entry to the Union. On August 21, 1959, he signed a proclamation that "admission of the State of Hawaii into the Union on an equal footing is now accomplished." And on July 4, 1960, the new flag with its official showing of fifty stars became official. On that day, with all its varied racial inheritances, girded by its long sandy beaches with their white combers, towered over by its volcanic mountains, covered in places by tropic jungles, with its thousands of square miles of sugar and of pineapple fields, Hawaii gave itself up to celebration. But only a tiny proportion of those who celebrated were of Hawaiian ancestry.

In the capital of Honolulu, on the island of Oahu, which had been the home of Hawaii's long line of kings, people gathered before the Iolani Palace where the kings had lived and which now houses the government, waving their leis, throwing their flowers, singing their songs. They were joined, as brothers in citizenship, by the white-coated American sailors, the khaki-clad American troops, the swaggering American fliers and the tens of thousands of American tourists who now make up the pattern of Honolulu. Each said to the other "Aloha."

INDEX

A

Alabama, 119, 126, 128-130
  source of name, 119, 129
Alamo, The, 91
Alaska, 136, 178-181
  source of name, 179-180
Albany, New York, 65
Allegheny River, 77
Allen, Ethan, 40-41
America, naming of, 15-18
Annapolis, Maryland, 51-52
Anne Arundel Town, Maryland, 51
Arapooish, Crow Indian Chief, 171
Argall, Samuel, 26, 61
Arizona, 87, 110-112
  source of name, 112
Arkansas, 118, 130-133
  source of name, 118
Arkansas River, 100, 132
Aroostook War, 36
Atlanta, Georgia, 57-58
Augusta, Maine, 36-37
Austin, Stephen, 91
Austin, Texas, 92-93

B

Balboa, Nuñez de, 19, 84
Baltimore, Lord (George Calvert), 50-51
Baltimore, Maryland, 51
Baton Rouge, Louisiana, 123
Bering, Vitus Jonassen, 178
Berkeley, Lord, 66
Bismarck, North Dakota, 166
Black Hawk War, 138
Block, Adrian, 42, 61
Boone, Daniel, 73, 74, 81, 97
Boise, Idaho, 168-169
Boston, Massachusetts, 32
Boston Tea Party, 33, 52
British Treaty of Independence, 77
Brown, John, 149
Bunyan, Paul, 145-146

C

Cabot, John, 20
California, 86-87, 92-97
  source of name, 93
California, Lower (Baja), 93
Calvert, Cecilius (Cecil), 51

186